Music in China

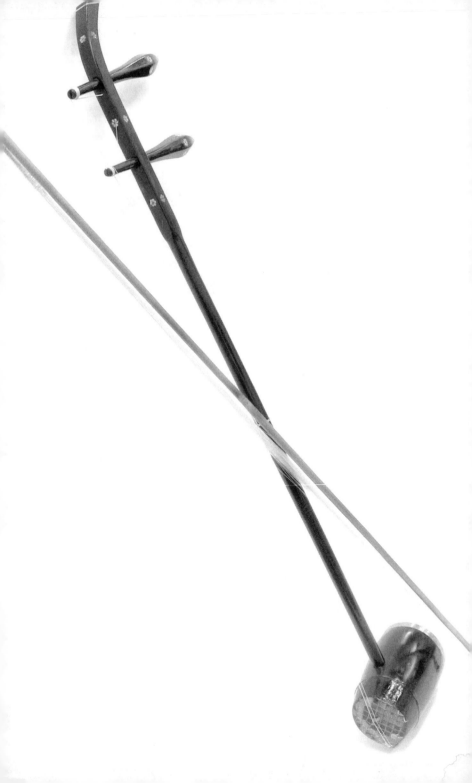

Music in China

∞

EXPERIENCING MUSIC, EXPRESSING CULTURE

∞

FREDERICK LAU

New York   Oxford
OXFORD UNIVERSITY PRESS
2008

Oxford University Press, Inc., publishes works that further Oxford University's
objective of excellence in research, scholarship, and education.

Oxford   New York
Auckland   Cape Town   Dar es Salaam   Hong Kong   Karachi
Kuala Lumpur   Madrid   Melbourne   Mexico City   Nairobi
New Delhi   Shanghai   Taipei   Toronto

With offices in
Argentina   Austria   Brazil   Chile   Czech Republic   France   Greece
Guatemala   Hungary   Italy   Japan   Poland   Portugal   Singapore
South Korea   Switzerland   Thailand   Turkey   Ukraine   Vietnam

Published by Oxford University Press, Inc.
198 Madison Avenue, New York, New York 10016
http://www.oup.com

Oxford is a registered trademark of Oxford University Press

Library of Congress Cataloging-in-Publication Data
Lau, Frederick.
   Music in China : experiencing music, expressing culture / Frederick Lau.
      p. cm. — (Global music series)
   Includes bibliographical references and index.
   ISBN-13: 978-0-19-530124-3 (paper (main))
   ISBN-13: 978-0-19-530123-6 (cloth)
  1. Music—China—History and criticism. I. Title.

ML336.L28 2008
780.951—dc22   2007014406

Printing number: 9 8 7 6 5 4 3 2 1

Printed in the United States of America
on acid-free paper

GLOBAL MUSIC SERIES

General Editors: Bonnie C. Wade and Patricia Shehan Campbell

Music in East Africa, Gregory Barz
Music in Central Java, Benjamin Brinner
Teaching Music Globally, Patricia Shehan Campbell
Native American Music in Eastern North America, Beverley Diamond
Carnival Music in Trinidad, Shannon Dudley
Music in Bali, Lisa Gold
Music in Ireland, Dorothea E. Hast and Stanley Scott
Music in China, Frederick Lau
Music in Egypt, Scott L. Marcus
Music in Brazil, John P. Murphy
Music in America, Adelaida Reyes
Music in Bulgaria, Timothy Rice
Music in North India, George E. Ruckert
Mariachi Music in America, Daniel Sheehy
Music in West Africa, Ruth M. Stone
Music in the Andes, Thomas Turino
Music in South India, T. Viswanathan and Matthew Harp Allen
Music in Japan, Bonnie C. Wade
Thinking Musically, Bonnie C. Wade

Contents

Foreword

∞

In the past three decades interest in music around the world has surged, as evidenced in the proliferation of courses at the college level, the burgeoning "world music" market in the recording business, and the extent to which musical performance is evoked as a lure in the international tourist industry. This heightened interest has encouraged an explosion in ethnomusicological research and publication, including production of reference works and textbooks. The original model for the "world music" course—if this is Tuesday, this must be Japan—has grown old, as has the format of textbooks for it, either a series of articles in single multiauthored volumes that subscribe to the idea of "a survey" and have created a canon of cultures for study, or single-authored studies purporting to cover world musics or ethnomusicology. The time has come for a change.

This Global Music Series offers a new paradigm. Instructors can now design their own courses; choosing from a set of case study volumes, they can decide which and how much music they will teach. The series also does something else; rather than uniformly taking a large region and giving superficial examples from several different countries within it, case studies offer two formats—some focused on a specific culture, some on a discrete geographical area. In either case, each volume offers greater depth than the usual survey. Themes significant in each instance guide the choice of music that is discussed. The contemporary musical situation is the point of departure in all the volumes, with historical information and traditions covered as they elucidate the present. In addition, a set of unifying topics such as gender, globalization, and authenticity occur throughout the series. These are addressed in the framing volume, *Thinking Musically* (Wade), which sets the stage for the case studies by introducing those topics and other ways to think about how people make music meaningful and useful in their lives. *Thinking Musically* also presents the basic elements of music as they are practiced in musical systems around the world so that authors of each case study do not have to spend time explaining them and can delve immediately into the particular music. A second framing volume, *Teaching Music*

Globally (Campbell), guides teachers in the use of *Thinking Musically* and the case studies.

The series subtitle, "Experiencing Music, Expressing Culture," also puts in the forefront the people who make music or in some other way experience it and also through it express shared culture. This resonance with global studies in such disciplines as history and anthropology, with their focus on processes and themes that permit cross-study, occasions the title of this Global Music Series.

Bonnie C. Wade
Patricia Shehan Campbell
General Editors

Preface

∞

Writing a book about Chinese music is a daunting task, especially considering the amount of available materials, its long and complex history, and its ever-changing musical soundscape. The decision of what to highlight undoubtedly rests on the writer's own musical encounter, experience, preference, and overall conception of the field. In *Music in China*, I address three enduring themes that deal with issues of identity, modernization, and ideology. Each of them contributed to shaping Chinese music in diverse ways and to providing the necessary conditions for the formation of new genres and styles. I selected a range of musical genres that are often subsumed under the general rubric of Chinese music not only to illustrate the themes but also to sketch a picture of what Chinese music entails for the majority of its insiders.

For a long time, music scholars inside and outside China have focused largely on the written traditions of the literati and the important role music played in elite culture while bypassing the music of commoners and the many popular folk genres. Substantial research on folk genres since the mid-twentieth century has opened up the world of folk, or *minjian* (literally, "among the folk"), music traditions and their important role in informing the theory and practice of all Chinese music. To present a more balanced representation of Chinese music, I chose themes that permit me to present genres of music performed by elite, local, and regional folk musicians; in academe; in the media; and on the concert stage inside and outside China.

As a performer of the Chinese bamboo flutes *dizi* and *xiao*, I have conducted research on various topics of Chinese music within China and in many overseas communities. I have taught courses on Chinese music and other world music at the university level for the last fifteen years. These diverse experiences have deepened my understanding of Chinese music and its impact on the people who have performed and have listened to it in the past. My students also taught me how best to present the materials and frame them in ways that are relevant to their lives. Their curiosity about and response to the material indirectly guided my choice of themes for this book.

Archaeological discoveries and written records confirm that Chinese music has a long history of at least seven thousand years. A sense of that history is constantly present in the minds of those who study it. However, this book avoids presenting Chinese music as a museumized tradition. Instead, it is presented as a dynamic music tradition that is performed and appreciated by contemporary audiences. This book cuts across time and space to include present-day Chinese music in China, in overseas Chinese communities, and in international settings. Chinese music culture, whether imagined, transplanted, or constructed, takes on particular meanings and implication in overseas Chinese communities in places such as Hong Kong, Taiwan, Singapore, San Francisco, Hawai'i, and Toronto.

This emphasis on the music's contemporary relevance also eschews the danger of presenting Chinese music as a monolithic tradition. It explains the processes that led, for example, to instruments of foreign origin such as the two-stringed bowed fiddle *erhu* and four-stringed plucked lute *pipa* becoming icons of Chinese music as well as to the Beijing opera—a regional music genre—being given the status of "national opera" in the early part of the twentieth century. Recognizing the changing nature of Chinese music, the importance of contexts that affect the emergence of new genres, and the resignification of older genres not only reveals the particular characteristics of Chinese music but also informs our sense of what comprises Chinese music.

Rather than viewing Chinese music as a coherent system of interrelated music categories, then, this book focuses on the musical features of selected genres, the processes through which they came into existence, and the sociopolitical relationships in their contexts. Like all other volumes in the Global Music Series, I avoid a chronological and descriptive approach. Rather, the interrelated themes act as narrative frames to guide the exploration of Chinese music as dynamic and multifaceted. The musical examples selected for discussion are appropriate for illustrating points; this is not intended to be a survey.

The first theme is identity of people and music. This is about a perception of what comprises "Chinese music" and what is identified as Chinese music according to different political and cultural contexts. During the Tang dynasty (618–907), Chinese music and practice were defined rather broadly. Considered by many music historians as a golden age of hybridized music, the cosmopolitan Tang dynasty incorporated various kind of foreign music, such as Indian, Korean, and Middle Eastern music, into its court music. At other times the identity and content of Chinese music incorporated mostly music of the Han, the ethnic group that comprises the majority. Perhaps the most drastic change in the identity of Chinese music occurred in the nineteenth century when European culture and music were imported into China through missionaries and the foreign military. Western music theory, ideals, instruments, and repertories began to infiltrate Chinese culture, providing alternatives and impetus for developing a new aesthetic. With the establishment of the People's Republic of China (PRC) in 1949, the identity of Chinese music again changed, this time by government-supported musicians to fit the then-newly promoted communist ideology. In stark contrast to upper-class music in the previous period, music since 1949 took on another new identity. With the process of creating a people's music and a national music with communist flavor firmly in place, new music genres and aesthetics once again were created. The identity of Chinese music continues to change since the economic reform of the late 1980s. In this volume, the body of pieces that defined Chinese music is examined in chapters 2 and 3 with discussions of national and regional genres.

The second theme deals with the responses to modernization and change as European music began to take root in Chinese music at the turn of the twentieth century. Whether or not we see Westernized Chinese music as "Chinese music," it is undeniable that Westernized Chinese music has become popular among most Chinese audiences. We can no longer simply view Chinese music as consisting only of traditional genres. After the introduction of European music in China, Chinese composers began to produce a large number of compositions in the styles of European models. Composers creatively blended Chinese elements into a mostly Western music frame and aesthetic, producing new styles of music that further pushed the limits that defined Chinese music. Contemporary media are yet another arena for contemporary creativity. New compositions, new kinds of national music, and a new generation of composers inside or outside China all now consider themselves to be writing Chinese music. The question for us is not to determine what is and what is not Chinese music, but to understand the dynamic processes to which Chinese musicians and listeners have responded.

The third theme, music and ideology, is a force that has influenced not only the identity but also the concept of music and musical practice for centuries. In ancient and modern China, music continues to play an important role in affirming and reinforcing ideology and social ethos. Since the time of the philosopher Confucius (551–479 B.C.E.), the classification of music into categories of *yayue* (elegant, refined music) and *suyue* (vernacular music that lacks moral restraints) has been in place with regard to different kinds of music. According to Confucianism, music, a necessary educational tool for scholars and the elite, was seen to have both positive and negative power. Playing the proper music was believed to enhance an individual's spiritual enlightenment and help maintain balance between individuals in order to arrive eventually at the pinnacle of Confucian ideal society—a harmonious world. In this sense, Confucius had a practical way of looking at music. This conception of music also affected how musicians practiced music and was indispensable in maintaining the centrality of Confucianism in Chinese society. Thus, for a long time, music has been in the forefront in upholding values and ideals. An extension of this kind of thinking can be found in the ubiquitous practice of music-making among the elite. We also see historical continuity in the role of music in communist China. With the establishment of the PRC government, a large number of music and music institutions were created to buttress and promote the newly promoted communist ideology. While this new ideology is a far cry from traditional Confucianist thinking, music has continued to be a medium through which ideology is being disseminated and maintained. Working together, these three themes function as lenses through which Chinese music is explored in this volume.

Acknowledgments

∞

The book is a result of many years of experience with Chinese music, beginning with accompanying my grandmother to watch Cantonese opera while growing up on Cheung Chau, a small island off the coast of Hong Kong. Although I never understood why she was attracted to the music, I was fascinated by her enthusiasm for what appeared to be an art form peculiar to her non-Cantonese native tongue. Growing up in then-colonial Hong Kong, I had the privilege of hearing different kinds of Chinese music performed live, on the radio, and on TV. These experiences directly and indirectly affected my attitude toward Chinese music. At the Chinese University of Hong Kong I first received my formal training in the subject. I owe much to my teachers Louis Chen, Bell Yung, Timothy Wilson, and Rulan Pian, who was a visiting scholar at the department at various times. From them, I learned what was given in the lectures and books, but more importantly, their insights into and nuanced reading of Chinese music exerted a huge impact on my thinking. In particular, Timothy Wilson, who is an excellent flute teacher and *xiao* player, opened many musical doors for me. I thank my teachers for their guidance.

While doing my dissertation research, I spent a year at the Shanghai Conservatory of Music. It was during that year I encountered Chinese music head on. My activities there ranged from interviewing musicians from across the country and taking lessons on *dizi, guqin,* and *xiao* to having classes with conservatory professors; attending academic conferences and performing with folk musicians; and discussing music with composers and officials. These encounters offered me a diverse view of what Chinese music meant to different constituents of the population. I wish to acknowledge all my informants and numerous scholars with whom I had contact. Specifically I want to thank my teachers Li Minxiong, Chen Yingshi, Tan Weiyu, Lu Chunling, Lin Yaoren, Wu Zhiming, the late Ye Dong, Chen Zhong, Yu Xunfa, and Tong Kequn for their generosity and willingness to share with me their views and material.

Throughout the years, I have benefited and received strong support from scholars outside China. I will start by acknowledging the nurturing and kindness of my teachers Bruno Nettl, Charlie Capwell, and Isabel Wong at the University of Illinois at Urbana-Champaign. In Hong Kong, Chan Sau Yan, Yu Siu Wah, Larry Witzleben, and Chan Hing Yan always made time for a conversation and allowed me to share my ideas. I owe much to the intellectual stimulation of Chinese music scholars in the United States and Europe. In particular, the work of Helen Rees, Su Zheng, Isabel Wong, Bell Yung, François Picard, Nancy Guy, Stephen Jones, Jonathan Stock, and Rachel Harris greatly enriched my understanding of specific areas of Chinese music about which I was ignorant. Special thanks go to Wing Tek Lum and Serge Tcherepnin for generously sharing photos and information about Alexander Tcherepnin. Thanks to pianist Thomas Yee and Bi-Chuan Li for recording their performance for the CD. I wish to thank my graduate students at the University of Hawai'i at Mānoa (UHM) for allowing me to try out some of the material for this book in classes and seminars and for challenging me to be succinct. I thank Sunhee Koo, Yinyee Kwan, Lee Ching Huei, Charlotte D'Evelyn, Will Connor, and Priscilla Puisze Tse for their openness in exploring new territory with me. A special note of thanks goes to Priscilla Tse for helping me locate the recordings and compiling them onto a CD. Her work has been professional and meticulous, and without her help this part of the project would have taken me considerably more time than originally estimated.

I'd also like to thank the reviewers of the manuscript: Lei Bryant, Skidmore College; Mercedes Dujunco, Bard College; Nancy Guy, University of California–San Diego; Tong Soon Lee, Emory University; Terry Miller, Kent State University; Rob Provine, University of Maryland; Margaret Sarkissian, Smith College; Yu Siu Wah, The Chinese University of Hong Kong; and Richard Wolf, Harvard University.

A special thanks to Bonnie Wade and Patricia Campbell, whose editorial suggestions and constant support are what every author wishes to have. Special thanks also go to Janet Beatty and Cory Schneider of Oxford University Press for their professional help. Last but not least, I would like to acknowledge the unfailing support of Heather Diamond, whose wit and intellectual insight sharpened my thinking and the clarity of my language. Her dedication to scholarly endeavors is a perfect pairing to the serene and aesthetically pleasing space she has created at home. To all of these people and to the many individuals I have forgotten to mention here, I am forever indebted to your generosity and support.

Note on Romanization, Chinese Names, and Chinese Cipher Notation

∞

All Chinese words in the text are rendered according to the pinyin system of romanization. This system, replacing the earlier Wade-Giles system, has become the standard used by the United Nations and most of the world's media since the 1980s. In this system, Roman letters are used to represent sounds in standard Mandarin. Exceptions are well-known names of places such as Peking (pinyin: Beijing), Hong Kong (pinyin: Xiang Gang), Canton (pinyin: Guangdong), and Hakka (pinyin: Kejia). In order to avoid confusion, I will use the names that are most commonly used in print and popular usage.

Following the Chinese convention, all Chinese names will first list the last name or family name, followed by a space and then the given name that contains either one or two characters. For the sake of iden-tification, all given names will appear without a space between the second and third character, for example: Cai Yuanpei, Mao Zedong, Liu Tianhua, and Tu Weiming. With regard to Chinese who were given English names, I will follow the way they are known in the West, such as Philip Huang, Rey Chow, David Chen, and Leo Lee.

Following the present-day convention of notating Chinese music, I adopt the simplified notation, or *jianpu*, in the text. The seven notes of a diatonic scale are represented by the numbers 1 to 7, and 0 is used to indicate rests. Note length is indicated by lines below the number. A number without any line is a quarter-note, one line underneath a note indicates an eighth-note, and two lines indicate a sixteenth-note. A dot after a note means that the note is prolonged by half its note-value. A dot can follow a note of any length. A dot above a note indicates an octave higher and dots below an octave lower. This notation also incorporates key and time signature, barline, slur, accidentals, tie, and expression markings that are used in Western music.

CD Track List

1. "Zhonghua liuban" ("Moderate Tempo Six Beats"). *Jiangnan sizhu,* excerpt. Field recording collected by author in Shanghai. August 1986.

2. "Jiangheshui" ("The Flow Water of Rivers and Streams"). Two-stringed bowed fiddle *erhu,* excerpt. From *Shanghai Spring Festival* (c. 1963). ROI: RB-011001-3C. 2001. Courtesy of ROI Productions (HK) Ltd.

3. "Caoyuanshang" ("On the Grassland"). Two-stringed middle-size bowed fiddle *zhonghu,* excerpt. From *Treasury of Chinese Musical Instruments.* Zhu Changyao (*zhonghu*). Decca: 421 011-2. 1987.

4. "Hangong qiuyue" ("Autumn Moon at the Han Palace"). Four-stringed pear-shaped plucked lute *pipa,* excerpt. Unpublished recording. Ho Kangming (*pipa*). 2004. Used by permission.

5. "Changmen yuan." ("Lament of Empress Chan"). Three-stringed plucked lute *sanxian,* excerpt. From *Ladies' Ensemble of Chinese Music.* Huang Guifang (*sanxian*). ROI: RA-961004C. 1996. Courtesy of ROI Productions (HK) Ltd.

6. "Babantou" ("Eight Beats Head"). Three-stringed round-shaped plucked lute *yueqin,* excerpt. Recorded for the author at Taipei University of the Arts, Taiwan. Huang Chinli (*yueqin*). November 14, 2006.

7. "Yingshanhong" ("The Red Ying Mountain"). Hammered dulcimer *yangqin,* excerpt. From *Riverside Scenes on Qing Ming Festival.* Liu Yuening (*yangqin*). BMG Pacific Ltd.: 8.242154. 1989.

8. "Gusuxing" ("A Trip to Suzhou"). Side-blown bamboo flute *dizi,* excerpt. From *Treasury of Chinese Musical Instruments.* Yu Xunfa (*dizi*). Decca: 421 011-2. 1987.

9. "Meihua sannong" ("Three Variations on the Plum Blossom Theme"). Vertical bamboo *xiao,* excerpt. From *Treasury of Chinese Musical Instruments.* Tan Weiyu (*xiao*). Decca: 421 011-2. 1987.

10. "Jin Diao" ("A Shanxi Province Melody"). Mouth organ *sheng*, excerpt. Live recording of a concert at the Inmin International Center, East-West Center, Honolulu. Loo Sze-wan (*sheng*). January 28, 2006. Used by permission.

11. "Bainiao chaofeng" ("Hundred Birds Flying toward the Phoenix"). Double-reed oboe *suona*, excerpt. From *Treasury of Chinese Musical Instruments.* Ren Tongxiang (*suona*). Decca: 421 011-2. 1987.

12. Example of arranged Chaozhou composition. Field recording by author.

13. "Xunfengqu." ("Fragrant Wind Tune"). Chaozhou *xianshi*, excerpt. Field recording collected by author in Shantou. 1992.

14. "Yaozu wuqu" ("Dance of the Yao People"). Chinese excerpt. From *The Repertoire of the National Orchestra of China.* The National Orchestra of China. ROI: RA-981010C. 1996. Courtesy of ROI Productions (HK) Ltd.

15. "Zhegufei" ("The Flight of the Partridge"). *Dizi* solo, excerpt. From *Announcing the Champions.* Dai Ya (*qudi*). ROI: RA-971015-C. 1994–1996. Courtesy of ROI Productions (HK) Ltd.

16. "Wubangzi" ("Five Clappers"). *Dizi* solo. From *Chinese Music Virtuosi* (Hong Kong). Unpublished recording. Chu Siu-wai (*bangdi*). 2004. Used by permission.

17. "Youyuan jingmeng." *Kunqu* opera *Peony Pavilion*, excerpt. From *Moudanting: Youyuan jingmeng.* Hua Wenyi (vocal). Yangzi yinxiang: ISRC CN-E03-02-0095-0/V.J8. Release year unknown.

18. "Erquan yingyue" ("Moon at Second Spring"). *Erhu* solo, excerpt. From *Commemoration of the Renowned Folk Musician.* Abing, Hua Yanqun (*erhu*, recorded in 1950). ROI: RC-961002-2C. 1996. Courtesy of ROI Productions (HK) Ltd.

19. "Shimian maifu" ("Ambush from All Sides"). *Pipa* solo, excerpt. From *Liu Dehai 50 Years in Music.* Liu Dehai (*pipa*). ROI: RC-011007-3C. 2001. Courtesy of ROI Productions (HK) Ltd.

20. "Yuzhou Wenchang" ("Evening Song of the Fisherman"). *Guzheng* solo, excerpt. From *Fantasia of River Miluo.* Fan Shang'e (*guzheng*). ROI: RB-951004C. 1995. Courtesy of ROI Productions (HK) Ltd.

21. "Shuang sheng han" ("Double Lament"). Cantonese instrumental music, excerpt. From *Commemoration of the Renowned Musician Loo Kah-chi.* Loo Kah-chi and the Hong Kong Cantonese Music Ensemble. ROI: RB-991006-2C. 1999. Courtesy of ROI Productions (HK) Ltd.

22. "Luoyan pingsha" ("The Geese Landing on the Flat Sand"). Cantonese instrumental music, excerpt (*suona* leads). From *The Martial Themes*. ROI: RB-961009C. 1996. Courtesy of ROI Productions (HK) Ltd.

23. "Fengxue yeguiren" ("Return at a Snowy Evening"). Cantonese opera *ping hou*, excerpt. From *Commemoration of the Renowned Musician Loo Kah-chi*. Loo Kah-chi and the Hong Kong Cantonese Music Ensemble. Xu Liuxian (*ping hou*). ROI: RB-991006-2C. 1999. Courtesy of ROI Productions (HK) Ltd.

24. "Zhuantai qiusi" ("Autumn Lament by the Vanity"). Cantonese opera *zi hou*, excerpt. From *Di nu hua* (Princess Chang Ping). Bai Xuexian (*zi hou*). Crown Records Co. Ltd. Hong Kong: CCD-2. Release date unknown.

25. "Zhouyu guitian" ("Zhouyu's Passing"). Cantonese opera *da hou*, excerpt. From *Commemoration of the Renowned Musician Loo Kah-chi*. Loo Kah-chi and the Hong Kong Cantonese Music Ensemble. Anonymous singer (*da hou*) ROI: RB-991006-2C. 1999. Courtesy of ROI Productions (HK) Ltd.

26. "Silang tanmu" ("The Fourth Son Visits His Mother"). Beijing opera *xipi liushui*, excerpt. From *Jingju silang tanmu*. Tong Zhiling and Guan Huai (vocal). Yangzi jiang yinxiang chubanshe: CN-F04-98-0027-0/V.J9. 1998.

27. *Jijifeng* ("A Gust of Wind"). Beijing opera percussion pattern, excerpt. Daniel Tschudi (*bangu*). Recorded for the author at the University of Hawai'i at Mānoa, Honolulu. 2006.

28. "Da jin zhuan" ("Striking the Golden Brick"). Beijing opera *erhuang manban laosheng* aria, excerpt. From *Yu Kuaizhi yanchu zhuanji Da jin zhuan*. Beijing dongfang yingyin gongsi: KZ-0001-VCD. 2000.

29. "Ye shen chen" ("Deep Night"). *Jinghu*, excerpt. From *Treasury of Chinese Musical Instruments*. Zhang Suying (*jinghu*). Decca: 421 011-2. 1987.

30. "Dongtian han" ("Winter Days Are Cold"). *Nanguan*, excerpt. From *Qingyin Yayun Huang Yaohui nanguan shanqu zhuanji*. Huang Yaohui (vocal). Unpublished recording. Taizhong: Liyuan yuefang. 2005.

31. "Zhonghua liu ban" ("Moderate Tempo Six Beats"). *Jiangnan sizhu Fangman jiahua*, excerpt. Live recording of a concert at the Inmin International Center, East-West Center, Honolulu. Chinese Music Virtuosi. January 28, 2006. Used by permission.

32. "Chuang jiangling" ("General's Command"). *Luogu* and *chuida,* excerpt. From *The Martial Themes.* Lu Chungling (conductor). ROI: RB-961009C. 1996. Courtesy of ROI Productions (HK) Ltd.

33. "Von der Jugend" ("Youth"). Excerpt. From Gustav Mahler's *Das Lied von der Erde (Song of the Earth).* Bruno Walter (conductor) and the Columbia Symphony Orchestra. MK: 42034. CBS Inc. 1960.

34. "Chinatown, My Chinatown." Thomas Yee (piano). Recorded for the author at the University of Hawai'i at Mānoa, Honolulu. December 12, 2006.

35. "Mutong duandi" ("A Shepherd's Flute"). Piano solo. Unpublished recording. Li Bichuan (piano).

36. "Yu ko" ("Fisherman's Song"). For violin, wind instruments, piano, and percussion by Chou Wen-Chung, excerpt. Courtesy of Chou Wen-Chung and Shyhji Pan-Chew, Canada and Taiwan Arts Exchange. 2004.

37. "Liushui" ("Flowing Water"). *Guqin* solo, excerpt. From *Favorite Qin Pieces of Guan Ping-hu.* Guan Ping-hu *(guqin).* ROI: RB-951005-2C. 1995. Courtesy of ROI Productions (HK) Ltd.

38. "Dialogue with 'Little Cabbage.'" By Tan Dun, excerpt. From *Ghost Opera for String Quartet and Pipa* (1994). Kronos Quartet and Wu Man *(pipa).* Nonesuch Records: 79445-2. 1997.

39. "Shuang Que" ("Double Watchtower"). Duo for *erhu* and *yanqin* by Tan Dun. From *Love of the Yangtze.* Ma Xianghua *(erhu),* Liu Yuening *(yangqin).* ROI: RA-981013C. 1998. Courtesy of ROI Productions (HK) Ltd.

40. "Ye Shanghai" ("Shanghai Night"). Early Chinese popular music, excerpt. From *Greatest Hits from the Last Century: 1930s and 1940s.* Zhou Xuan (vocal). China Record Shanghai Co.: CN-E01-00-406-00/A.J6. 2001.

41. "Langzhi hui tou" ("Vagabond's Desires"). *Cantopop,* excerpt. From *Selected Golden Hits of Sam Hui koon-kit, 2 Volumes.* Sam Hui (vocal). PolyGram Records Ltd. HK: 513 214-2 (513 216-2). 1992.

42. "Herijun zailai" ("When Will the Gentleman Come Again?"). Mandarin song, excerpt. From *Teresa Teng xianyan wanyu sujunqing.* Teresa Teng (vocal). Taiwan Ming Yueh Records Co, Ltd.: MY-1002. 2003.

43. "Yiwu suoyou" ("I Have Nothing"). Chinese rock music, excerpt. From *Cui Jian Yiwu suoyou.* Cui Jian (vocal). Coden Records (Taiwan) Ltd.: CD-85093. 1994.

44. "Menggu Ren" ("Mongols"). Excerpt. From *Teng Ge'er Menggu Ren*. Teng Ge'er (vocal). Zhongxin Records, Guangzhou, PRC: CN-F21-99-329-00/A.J6. 2002.

45. Historical recording of Confucian ritual, c. 1925. Collected by the author.

46. "Shanpo yang." ("The Goat on the Slope"). Naxi music, excerpt. From *Naxi Ancient Music*. Lijiang Zhongguo Dayan Naxi guyuehui. Shanghai yinxiang: ISRC CN-E07-98-331-00/A.J6. 1998.

47. "Dongfang Hong" ("East Is Red"). Revolutionary mass song, excerpt. From *The East Is Red Collection*. Guangzhou xin shidai yingyin: ISRC CN-F21-99-383-00/A.J6. 1999.

48. "Wo ai Beijing de Tiananmen" ("I Love Beijing's Tiananmen"). Revolutionary mass song, excerpt. From *The East Is Red Collection*. Guangzhou xin shidai yingyin: ISRC CN-F21-99-383-00/A.J6. 1999.

49. "Baimaonu" ("White-Haired Girl"). Model opera *Yangbanxi*, excerpts. From *Modern Ballet: White-Haired Girl*. Zhu Fengbo (vocal). ROI: ISRC CN-A05-94-0010-0/V.17. 1994. Courtesy of ROI Productions (HK) Ltd.

50. "Two Flowers on a Stem." Chinese-American jazz, excerpt. From *Two Flowers on a Stem*. Jon Jang (piano). Soul Note: 121253-2. 1996.

51. "Tian mi mi." ("Sweet Like Honey"). Thai-Chinese singing club, excerpt. Field recording collected by the author. 1995.

52. "Chusaiqu" ("Song of Leaving the Border"). Chinese choral music, excerpt. Han Sheng Choir, Honolulu. Recorded for the author at the Orvis Auditorium, University of Hawai'i at Mānoa, Honolulu. September 12, 2004.

53. "Miracle." Modern Chinese music, excerpt. From *Beautiful Energy*. Twelve Girls Band. Universal Music Limited and Platia Entertainment Inc.: 476-166-8. 2003.

CHAPTER 1

Music of the People

FIRST ENCOUNTER: TEAHOUSE MUSIC IN THE JIANGNAN AREA

It was an early September evening in 1986 when I first visited Shanghai's Hu Xing Ting, "Pavilion in the Middle of the Lake" (Figure 1.1). As a newcomer to the city where I would be conducting research at the Shanghai Conservatory, I had been invited to attend a musical event celebrating the Mid-Autumn Festival. Nestled in the bustling "old city" of Shanghai (Figure 1.2), Hu Xing Ting was erected during the Ming dynasty (1368–1644 c.e.). Now a public teahouse, the old hexagonal building is a must-see for tourists as an important historic landmark that embodies Shanghai's colorful and vibrant history. This beautiful, ornate, two-story structure is built at the side of a small manmade lake facing the back walls of the classic Yu Yuan Garden at the opposite side; the pavilion and the garden are connected by a footbridge zigzagging across the lake. The tranquillity of the classic garden poses a stark contrast to glittering Shanghai's modern attractions and the noise coming from the bustling surrounding neighborhood where I had to navigate small alleyways. Finally, I arrived at an open space where the pavilion was in full view. Hand-painted paper lanterns hung from the upper-floor windows. As I approached the teahouse, the sound of traditional string and wind instruments could be heard. I had no idea that this evening would open the door to the world of communal amateur music-making that changed my experience and understanding of Chinese music forever.

The second floor of Hu Xing Ting was one big, open, circular space defined by small tables and chairs arranged along the walls and next to the windows. Guests were already seated along the perimeter of the room, socializing, chatting, and leisurely drinking tea. In the center of the room sat a marble-topped, redwood table surrounded by stools. A *yangqin* (hammered dulcimer) was set up on one side of the table

FIGURE 1.1 *Shanghai's Hu Xing Ting, "Pavilion in the Middle of the Lake."* *(Photo by Lei Ouyang Byrant, 2005)*

at the far end from where I was sitting. On the open surface of the table was a collection of beautifully lacquered and somewhat seasoned strings, winds, and percussion, instruments for playing *jiangnan sizhu* music.

As soon as all the guests settled down in their places, an official-looking man stood up and welcomed everyone in the Shanghai dialect that, at the time, I struggled to understand. I later found out that it is a custom that welcome speeches are necessary for most public events, including concerts and plays. He then invited players to come to the table and asked each player to select an instrument. Once all the instrumentalists took their seats around the table, they started to tune the instruments, taking a note from the flute player. In few polite exchanges, the musicians selected the pieces and, not before long, the percussionist struck two preparation beats and the music began. This type of local ensemble music is called *jiangnan sizhu*—literally, "silk and bamboo music"—and is from south of the Yangtze

FIGURE 1.2 *Map of China.*

River around the city of Shanghai (Figure 1.3). *Silk* is an ancient term referring to all string instruments because strings used to be made of silk. *Bamboo,* the material for all wind instruments, is the term for all wind instruments. *Jiangnan* refers to the area in east central China that is famous for its moderate weather, abundance of produce, mulberry, bamboo, and beautiful scenery.

CD track 1, recorded during my fieldwork in Shanghai, is a fine example of *jiangnan sizhu* music in the teahouse. The combination of bowed and plucked strings provided a perfect balance of articulating and sustaining sound for the music to a Western-trained musician like myself. Accentuated by the gentle beats alternating between the flat drum *bangu* and handheld wooden clapper, the music was smooth and even, offering an unusual countermelody to the continuous ambiance noise in the room. Because slightly different versions of the melody were being played simultaneously (heterophonic texture), it was at times difficult to distinguish each instrument individually. The ensemble was made up of a combination of chordophones, aerophones, and idiophones (see the following discussion). I discovered that the number

FIGURE 1.3 Jiangnan sizhu, *"silk and bamboo" ensemble, CD track 1. From left to right clockwise:* pipa, yangqin, erhu, dizi, sheng, bangu *and* clapper, erhu, erhu, *and* qinqin. *2006. (Courtesy of Frederick Lau)*

of players was flexible and the size of the ensemble could expand or contract, depending on who was available. I later learned that this flexibility is typical of silk and bamboo music.

Chordophones. The bowed and plucked strings in this ensemble are two kinds of chordophone, an instrument in which a vibrating string produces the sound. *Erhu* and *zhonghu* (Figure 1.4), the two most important bowed strings in *jiangnan sizhu,* are similar in structure but different in size. *Erhu,* also known as *huqin* ("barbarian lute"), is an instrument imported into China via the Silk Road trade that has been sinicized over the years. Despite its origins as an imported instrument, as indicated by the label *hu* (a word the Chinese used to mean "barbarian"), this instrument has come to represent the sonic signature of Chinese music, especially with its characteristic glissando. The *erhu* is a two-stringed fretless bowed instrument that is tuned to the interval of a fifth, but the actual pitches vary according to region and style of music

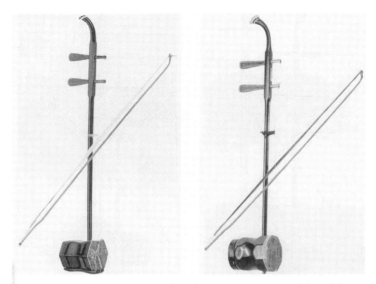

FIGURE 1.4   Erhu *(left) and* zhonghu *(right) (two-stringed bowed lutes),* CD tracks 2 and 3. Also known as huqin, *their construction consists of a round and fretless pole mounted perpendicular to a small round or hexagonal-shape resonating chamber, covered on one end with snakeskin. The bow, made of horse hair, is placed between the two strings. Sound is produced by pushing or pulling the bow against the inner or outer string. Common tunings are D-A, C-G, or A-D. Different varieties of* huqin *can be found across the country, and many are still being used in regional music traditions. Among them are the Chaozhou* erxian, *Beijing Opera* jinghu, *Cantonese* gaohu *and* yehu, *northern Chinese* banhu, *Shaanxi* sihu, *and Fujian* tixian. *(Courtesy of Frederick Lau)*

(CD track 2). The slightly larger *zhonghu* is played with a technique similar to that of the *erhu*. Tuned an octave lower than the *erhu*, the *zhonghu* is often used as a secondary instrument to provide a thicker sound complement or texture to the high-pitched *erhu* (CD track 3). Because of its mellow tone quality, the *zhonghu* is often used as a supporting instrument in the modern Chinese orchestra (chapter 2). The collection of plucked chordophones in this ensemble includes *pipa* (Figure 1.5, CD track 4), *sanxian* (Figure 1.6, CD track 5), *yueqin* (Figure 1.7, CD track 6), and *yangqin* (Figure 1.8, CD track 7). These instruments are discussed in more detail in the figure captions.

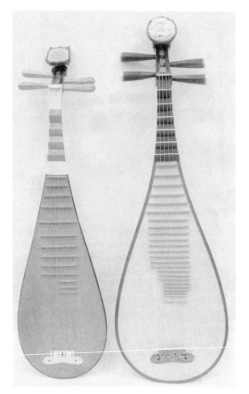

FIGURE 1.5   Pipa *(four-stringed fretted lute),
CD track 4. A pear-shaped fretted lute, the* pipa *is
held upright and played with finger picks attached to
the righthand fingers. According to pictorial evidence,
the* pipa *is thought to have been imported to China
via the Silk Road, and its history can be dated before
the Tang dynasty (618–907) during the sixth century. (Courtesy of Yu Siuwah)*

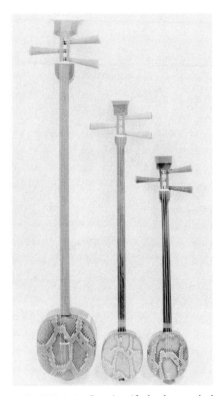

FIGURE 1.6 Sanxian *(fretless long-necked lute)*, *CD track 5. The* sanxian *is a three-string plucked instrument with a snakeskin membrane stretched over a small rectangular sound box. Because of its rich tonal quality and wide range, the* sanxian *is widely used for accompaniment, orchestral, and solo performances. The* sanxian *is made in three sizes: large, medium, and small. The large one is used mainly for accompanying storytelling, narrative songs, and musical drama performances. (Courtesy of Yu Siuwah)*

FIGURE 1.7 Yueqin *(short-necked lute)*, *CD track 6. Also known as the moon lute, the* yueqin *has a fretted short neck and round flat box as its resonator. The four strings are arranged into two pairs, each pair called a course. The two courses are tuned an octave apart, and the two strings in each course are tuned a fourth or fifth apart. Most players prefer to use only two strings. The instrument is plucked with a thin plectrum and has a clear and vibrant tone quality. The* yueqin *is often played with other plucked instruments and is seldom played as a solo instrument. (Courtesy of Yu Siuwah)*

FIGURE 1.8   Yangqin *(hammered dulcimer), CD track 7. The* yangqin *is another imported instrument. Its origin can be traced back to the Ming dynasty around the sixteenth century. The earliest type of* yangqin *had two rows of bridges atop the box, each supporting eight to twelve courses (two strings per course). The preferred style of* yangqin *for* jiangnan sizhu *and most regional music traditions is the one seen here. Since the mid-1950s, the* yangqin *has been further developed by adding more rows and strings in order to increase its volume, pitch, range, and chromatic capability. The new models have been expanded to three rows with ten courses each or four rows with twelve or thirteen courses each. Sustaining pedals, similar to those found on pianos, are also installed to control the volume and duration of sustaining pitches. Special tuning devices such as the grooves with balls on both sides were added for the convenience in modulating. Newly designed bamboo beaters with plastic tips have been created to temper the harshness when the bamboo strikes the strings. (Courtesy of Frederick Lau)*

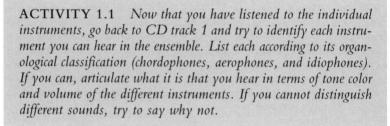

FIGURE 1.9 Dizi *(side-blown flute), CD track 8. The side-blown bamboo flute is also known as a di or zhudi (bamboo flute). It is made of a piece of bamboo with six finger holes, a blow hole, and an extra hole located between the blow hole and the first finger hole for the placement of a thin membrane. The nasal timbre caused by the vibrating membrane is perhaps the most distinctive character of the dizi. The average range of the dizi is about two and half octaves, and it comes in different lengths. The moderate-length dizi used in* jiangnan sizhu *is called a* qudi *and is tuned to the key of D. (Courtesy of Yu Siuwah)*

Aerophones. The three aerophones in a *jiangnan sizhu* ensemble are the side-blown bamboo flute *dizi* (Figure 1.9, CD track 8), the vertical notched flute *xiao* (Figure 1.10, CD track 9), and the mouth organ *sheng* (Figure 1.11, CD track 10). The *dizi* is considered the leading instrument of the ensemble, while the *xiao* and *sheng* mostly play a less complicated version of the main melody. Since *jiangnan sizhu* is performed mostly indoors, the loud double reed shawm *suona* (Figure 1.12, CD track 11) is not used in the ensemble. Because the aerophones and chordophones in the *jiangnan sizhu* ensemble are used in other music discussed in this book, the reader is advised to memorize the information about them now.

Idiophones. In this ensemble, *bangu* (Figure 1.13) and a pair of wooden clappers (also Figure 1.13) are the two main idiophones, instruments whose primary sound-producing medium is the body of the instrument itself. Played by one person, these two instruments function as a tempo and dynamic leader. Occasionally a pair of small bells are used to add a layer of festive atmosphere to the music.

ACTIVITY 1.1 *Now that you have listened to the individual instruments, go back to CD track 1 and try to identify each instrument you can hear in the ensemble. List each according to its organological classification (chordophones, aerophones, and idiophones). If you can, articulate what it is that you hear in terms of tone color and volume of the different instruments. If you cannot distinguish different sounds, try to say why not.*

FIGURE 1.10   Xiao *(vertical flute)*, *CD track 9.*
The xiao *is a vertical-notched bamboo flute with*
four or five finger holes in the front and one in the
back. Unlike its southern counterpart dongxiao
in Fujian and Guangdong provinces, the xiao
has a narrow body and a delicate timbre. Its range
is about two octaves. In its early history, the xiao
was used in Confucian ritual and frequently
appeared with the seven-stringed plucked chordo-
phone qin. *1986. (Courtesy of Frederick Lau)*

I found this music, with its lyricism and moderato tempo, easy to
listen to and the music-making interesting to watch because the musicians all played from memory. The main melody was clearly identifiable because the whole ensemble was simultaneously playing a version
of its melodic variations (CD track 1). I noticed that the *dizi* player was
leading the ensemble and playing a particularly elaborate version of the
melody. The pieces I heard that night started with a moderate tempo
and gradually accelerated to a climactic ending.

When the first group of players had played two pieces, they returned
to their seats and the same man came out and invited another group
of players to the table. In the course of the evening, almost everyone
in the room had a chance to play except a few newcomers to the city.
I noticed that the same piece sounded slightly different from one

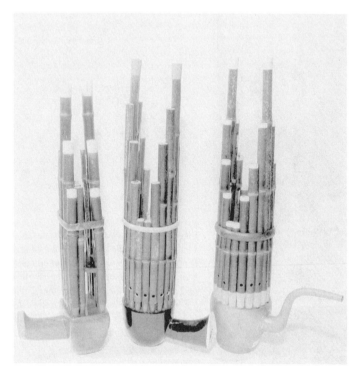

FIGURE 1.11 Sheng *(mouth organ), CD track 10. According to archaeological evidence, the mouth organ* sheng *is one of the oldest Chinese wind instruments. It is the only Chinese wind instrument capable of producing two or more tones simultaneously. The* sheng *is made up of a bundle of bamboo pipes of various lengths mounted on a small gourd-shaped wind chamber. A thin brass reed is attached to the end of each bamboo pipe before it is inserted inside the wind chamber. Sound is produced by blowing and sucking the air through a wooden or metal tube connected to the base and by closing the holes on selected pipes. The* sheng *is a versatile instrument that is used in many regions as both a solo and an accompaniment instrument. (Courtesy of Yu Siuwah)*

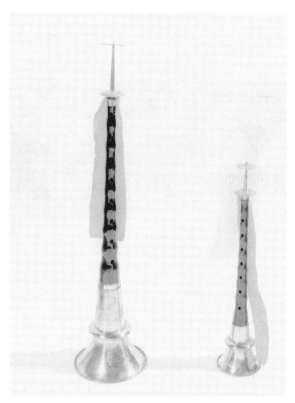

FIGURE 1.12 Suona, *CD track 11. A double-reed aerophone similar to a* shawm, *an instrument that has a plate on which the lips rest. Like most Chinese wind instruments, a* suona *comes in various sizes. It is used mainly in outdoor ensembles and processions. (Courtesy of Yu Siuwah)*

group to another. Without knowing much about the repertory and performance practice, I could hear from the playing that the individual players contributed tremendously to how the piece sounded by adding embellishments, altering the melody, subtracting or adding notes, and changing octaves. Even the same piece sounded differently when played by a different group of musicians. The evening ended with a long piece called "*Sihe ruyi*" ("Four Together, as You Please"), which I later learned is the most important piece of the entire repertory.

FIGURE 1.13   *Chinese percussion instruments. From left to right: little* gong xiaoluo
(handheld and mounted), big gong daluo *(hanging), small bells* pengling, *clappers* ban,
a pair of knobbed cymbals naobo *(on the floor), and two drums* gu *(*dagu *and* tang gu*)*
1987. (Courtesy of Frederick Lau)

Because the evening was a celebration of the Mid-Autumn Festival,
there were plenty of snacks available in the teahouse, such as moon
cakes, fruits, peanuts, and melon seeds. However, the performance of
music remained the primary focus throughout the evening. The event
didn't finish until past midnight, when I thanked my host and told him
I would be back. When asked where I could hear the music again, the
musicians told me to come back to the same location every Monday
afternoon when they would play *jiangnan sizhu* music.

As a performer of Western music, I was especially intrigued by this
music—its aesthetic and its practice—because it was so drastically different from the systematic, methodical, and regimental approach to music
propagated at the conservatory. After that evening, I became a regular
participant at the Hu Xing Ting music club on Mondays. As the musicians came to know me, they introduced me to the different teahouses
and the network of teahouse musicians around the city. Intrigued by
the music and environment, I began to pay regular visits to all the
teahouses that were recommended by my contacts during my stay in
Shanghai. In these venues, I met people from all walks of life, from

local resident and neighborhood musicians to tourists who happened to venture in. All were welcome to enter the space to listen to the music and to have a cup of tea. Set against the exclusive nature of an official music institution and my observations at the Shanghai Conservatory, the music in the teahouse revealed the dichotomy between the worlds of professional *zhuanye* music versus amateur *minjian* music in modern Chinese music.

ACTIVITY 1.2 *Listen to CD track 1 multiple times and focus on these elements of the music:*

1. *Focus on the changing density and take note of the timing of any change you hear.*

2. *Listen for the tempo of the music and likewise note the moments of change.*

3. *Note the timing and nature of the interesting interplay between the* dizi *and the* erhu.

4. *Make a composite listening chart based on your observation of the three elements.*

After you have completed all four activities, exchange listening charts with one classmate to compare what you hear. Together, answer this question: Do you hear changes in dynamics (louder or softer volume) in this piece?

SECOND ENCOUNTER: *XIANSHI* IN CHAOZHOU REGION

My musical encounter in Shanghai left me wanting to experience amateur music-making in other areas. On a later trip to China in 1992, I traveled to the south China city of Shantou (Figure 1.2), the capital of Chaozhou region, which is situated in the northeastern coastal part of Guangdong (Canton) province. Chaozhou is famous for its unique regional culture, multiple dialects in one region, and music, all of which are drastically different from those found elsewhere in the province. One of the popular musical styles in the Chaozhou region is a type of string ensemble music called *xianshi*, performed mostly by amateurs for their own amusement. The purpose of my trip was to learn firsthand what this music was like and how it differed from Shanghai teahouse music. What I encountered in this region provided me with more insights about amateur music-making in contemporary China.

I arrived in Shantou in the middle of the summer. The intense summer heat and humidity added a certain clutter to the already crowded and ever-changing urban landscape. The city was lively, the shops loudly blasting Hong Kong and Taiwanese Chinese popular songs and American-style soft rock. The Chaozhou region had been designated by the government as a special economic zone in the 1980s when the government adopted economic reform across the country. Shantou had become the hub of all cultural and economic activities of the entire Chaozhou region. Overseas investments and business poured in, prompting a massive inflow of capital, people, and various popular cultural forms to the region, especially from Hong Kong, Taiwan, and Singapore.

I informed my host of my desire to listen to local Chaozhou music. To my surprise, I was taken to the office of the Chaozhou Song and Dance Troupe. This troupe, fully supported by the Ministry of Culture, is the most important official music organization in the region. To my utter amusement, what I encountered was not what I had expected. After the initial introduction, I was led into a big rehearsal hall with chairs and music stands set up on a stage for a big orchestra. The musicians filed in and took their seats. Then they proceeded to open their music folders and instrument cases and tune up. The conductor stepped up to the podium and gave a downbeat with his baton, and the orchestra began to play (CD track 12).

Contrary to the amateur music-making session at the Shanghai teahouse, the ensemble was led by a conductor and the music was composed and arranged. The careful orchestration, exaggerated dynamic differences, and tempo changes immediately recalled Western symphonic music and practice. Although the music was based on a traditional Chaozhou theme, the texture departed greatly from the heterophonic texture heard in *jiangnan sizhu* (CD track 1) and relied mostly on Western harmony as its basis. Throughout the forty-five-minute performance, I did not notice any music that was different from the professional traditional Chinese orchestral music that I had heard at the Shanghai Conservatory and at the Shanghai Traditional Chinese Orchestra. After the concert, the conductor introduced me to the resident composer and arranger of the music. They told me that these were the best-known Chaozhou pieces of the region and that they were an improvement on the music performed by the *minjian* music groups, voluntary amateur folk music groups that are not financially supported and musically scrutinized by the government. As a result, I was determined to find out how those pieces were different from those played by the *minjian* musicians.

ACTIVITY 1.4 *Compare and contrast the piece on CD track 12 to the style of* jiangnan sizhu *on CD track 1. What can you say about the main differences between the two styles in terms of the same musical details?*

Dissatisfied with what had been shown to me, I decided to venture out by myself to see what I could find. As luck would have it, early one morning I stumbled onto a park in the middle of the city and heard music being piped out of a few loudspeakers in the distance. Not too far from one of the side entries to the park, I saw a bamboo structure that was shaped like a stage with chairs placed in front of it. Sitting to the side of the stage, a group of musicians was playing various traditional instruments, accompanying two female singers who were standing in the middle of the stage and performing for a small audience. The music they were performing was drastically different from the music I had heard in the orchestral practice room a few days earlier. The music was not precomposed or arranged, the overall sound quality of the music was nasal, and the texture was heterophonic, with the instrumentalists performing variants of the same tune. The singer as well occasionally added embellishments and interludes to enrich the texture and dynamics. I stayed to ask the musicians about the music and ways of performing the music. "This music was Chaozhou *xianshi,*" explained one musician, "the most popular string ensemble of this region. The leading instrument in *xianshi* is the high-pitched and nasal bowed lute—*erxian*" (literally, "two strings"; see Figures 1.14 and 1.15).

 FIGURE 1.14 Erxian, *CD track 13. This bowed chordophone is a variant of the* huqin *family. It produces a tense and piercing timbre. The resonator of the* erxian *is a small round wooden cylinder rather than the hexagonal-shaped resonator found on an* erhu. *(Courtesy of Yu Siuwah)*

FIGURE 1.15 *Chaozhou* xianshi *ensemble, CD track 13. The instrumentation is similar to that of* jiangnan sizhu *except that there are no aerophones in the ensemble and the leading instrument is the* erxian. *From left to right:* erxian, sanxian, pipa, yangqin, erhu, *and* yueqin. *1995. (Courtesy of Frederick Lau)*

Although the appearance and playing technique of the *erxian* are similar to those of an *erhu,* its piercing and harsh timbre give *xianshi* music a unique sonic signature (CD track 13). Through this initial contact, I was introduced to the world of amateur *minjian* music-making in the city.

ACTIVITY 1.5 *The tone quality and color of* erxian *contribute significantly to the overall sound of* xianshi *music. But if you listen to* jiangnan sizhu *again, you will hear a different kind of sound emerge because the leading sound is produced by the* dizi, *which gives the ensemble a unique sonority as opposed to that of the* erxian. *How does the overall sound of the selection on CD track 13 compare to that of* jiangnan sizhu *on CD track 1, and how did the*

two leading instruments affect the tone color of the ensemble? If you were to describe the sounds of these two genres to someone who has not heard this music before, what would you say? Think about how this music conforms to and contrasts with your stereotypical notions of Chinese music, and why, in terms of sound.

Similar to the music clubs that play in Shanghai teahouses, the music clubs in Shantou often gather mostly in informal public venues with informal settings, such as social clubs, neighborhood recreational centers, community halls, parks, and private homes. The atmosphere is relaxed and informal compared to a formal concert presentation. There are usually two main types of people in the room: musicians and audience members. The musicians, sitting close to the center of the room, are most likely to be asked by the host to play. A round of playing consists of two or three pieces, and musicians take turns performing and listening. Instrumentalists who participate in the music clubs are mostly male, as in most traditional music practice. As a prevalent practice based on gender and class across China, women were mostly singers rather than instrumentalists. This may be related to the fact that Confucianism considered music and instrumental playing part of a scholar's education (see chapter 5). Although not all professional instrumentalists came from a scholarly background, men were often affiliated with instrumental playing based on the Confucianist thinking. However, this trend has changed in the last several decades when large numbers of women began to enter the professional world of instrumental music performance.

Professional musicians in general do not participate in these *minjian* activities. According to one informant, this is because of the differences in musical practice, aesthetics, and social status between professional and amateur musicians. Even though professional musicians are commonly recognized as better trained, their knowledge of the traditional repertory, performance practice, and nuanced and proficient playing technique are regarded by many local musicians as inadequate and their musical taste and flexibility as inferior to those of the amateurs.

There is a group feeling about the gatherings where music is heard in Shantou. The audience mostly consists of friends, music lovers, and neighbors who enjoy listening to this particular music. They feel at ease socializing while the music is being played in the background. As is common practice in social gatherings in the Chaozhou region, a very strong local black tea prepared in Chaozhou style is served along with various local snacks. In private homes and invited sessions, Chaozhou food such as rice porridge and snacks is sometimes served after the performance. Taken as a whole, the performance of music with local flavors is more than a musical event. It is an expression of a regional identity.

In many townships and counties of Chaozhou, the local amateur *minjian* music activities seemed to be flourishing and well supported. These voluntary musical activities have been on the rise since the government relaxed its cultural policies in the 1980s (see the timeline of Chinese history). In all the places I visited in this region, there seemed to be a well-developed network of music clubs and musicians within each area. In the small town of Chenghai not far from Shantou, for example, an informant told me that there were at least nine to ten music clubs in a twenty-kilometer radius and that one could easily find *xianshi* music being played every night. My informant was right. During my short stay in the small town of Chenghai, I visited four different clubs and was invited to participate in the opening ceremony of a newly established music club in the outskirts of Chenghai. Many musicians remarked that in the last several years there has been considerable interest and public support in reviving local musical traditions. This growing interest in regional Chaozhou music by local musicians is similar to what has happened to *jiangnan sizhu* in Shanghai.

Timeline of Chinese History

Dynasty	Western Dates
Xia	*c. Twenty-first to sixteenth centuries* B.C.E.
Shang	*1700–1027*
Western Zhou	*1027–771*
Eastern Zhou	*770–221*
Spring and Autumn period	*770–476*
Warring States period	*475–221*
Qin	*221–207*
Han	*202* B.C.E.*–220* C.E.
Wei, Jin, Northern, and Southern	*220–581*
Sui	*581–618*

Tang	618–907
Five Dynasties and Ten Kingdoms	907–959
Song	960–1279
Yuan	1279–1368
Ming	1368–1644
Qing	1644–1911
Republic period	1912–1949
PRC	1949–present

Traditionally, Chinese dates were identified first by the dynasty, then by the "reign name" of the particular emperor, and finally by the year within the reign. For example, Qing dynasty, Guangxu reign, twenty-ninth year is the equivalent of 1903 in the Western calendar.

Based on my visits in Shanghai and Chaozhou, I was convinced that amateur *minjian* music-making is alive and well in the People's Republic of China (PRC) despite the many government-supported performing troupes across the country in every province. I continued my journey to locate more amateur music in the nearby Hakka area, another dialect group in the neighboring northeastern mountain region (Figure 1.2). The flourishing local amateur music scene I found there was rather strikingly similar to my observations in other regions. These musical encounters gave me a good picture of the current status of traditional Chinese music at the local level vis-à-vis that of government-sponsored music institutions.

Chaozhou music is supported not only by local musicians but also by overseas Chaozhounese. For example, most of the funding for Chaoyue Yanjiushe (The Association of Chaozhou Music Research), perhaps the most prestigious club in Chenghai, has been provided by overseas Chaozhounese from Hong Kong and Thailand, where some of its musicians have been invited to perform and teach. Unlike other clubs that practice in public places, this club has its own location and, apart from weekly practice sessions, also sponsors instrumental classes. With increasing popularity outside China, Chaozhou *xianshi* music has extended its reputation to become a cultural icon of Chaozhou identity.

AMATEUR MUSIC-MAKING IN THE PRC

Like most people, I was surprised to discover that amateur music-making continued to be practiced in contemporary China in the 1980s.

Before arriving there, I was under the impression that this kind of grassroots musical practice had become something of the past because of urbanization and the centralized cultural policies of the communist government since 1949. After the establishment of the PRC, the Chinese Communist Party (CCP) forged a new political and cultural policy based on the socialist doctrines of Lenin, Marx, and Mao. To ensure its success, reforms in all realms of societies were carried out under the direction of the centralized government. In music and other performing arts, this included the popularization of mass music, the creation of new musical genres that reflected the appropriate political ideology, and the building of music institutions and performing troupes. In the process, many traditional practices were abandoned, transformed, or suppressed because they conflicted with the dominant political ideology.

Amateur music-making, however, has not been eradicated by the advent of popular entertainment and the media or by the intense economic development program and drastic social changes since the 1980s. What I saw in Shanghai and Chaozhou raised several questions: What was continuing to motivate people to participate in this form of music-making? What is the Chinese government's attitude toward amateur musicians? And why should a government's attitude and policy matter to musicians?

In prerevolutionary China, the distinction between amateur and professional music was based mostly on a long and complex history involving social class and ideology rather than the quality and skill of musicians. Amateur musicians pursued music for its ethical and educational functions, eschewing its sensuous or emotional qualities. Amateur musicians were members of the literati and educated men of leisure, the top rank of society in accordance with Confucian ideology. According to Confucian ideology, a member of the literati class is an educated and intellectual elite who possesses the moral faculty, ethics, and knowledge to contribute to the creation of a harmonious world. Professional musicians in China were of low social status because Confucianism placed literati in the top rank of society and all other persons lower in social status. This particular stratification of society, produced and maintained by the literati, privileged the ethical and educational functions of music while discrediting its social significance as well as its sensuous and emotional qualities. Professional musicians were considered low class because they provided service-oriented activities for social functions or entertainment. In the imperial periods such as the Han (202 B.C.E.–220 C.E.) and Tang (618–907 C.E.) dynasties, court musicians were known disparagingly as "music labor" or "music craftsmen" (*yuegong* or *yuexiang*), and their job was to provide ceremonial and entertainment music for the nobility and aristocracy. This negative attitude toward working musicians continued and extended to other secular and vernacular music when popular literature and entertainment began to gain attention beyond the court and integrate with the lives of common people during the Song dynasty (960–1279 C.E.). In short, while professional musicians provided a much-needed service to society, they were low class in comparison to literati and were scorned by the majority of the society.

In the system they produced, then, scholars and literati placed their own involvement in musical activities into the amateur category. An amateur was someone whose musical endeavor was intended for cultivating one's character and morality rather than for dealing with practical matters such as making money or earning. By claiming to be amateur musicians, they distinguished themselves from working musicians known as *yiren* (literally, "artistic person"), thereby protecting their superior social status. This unique perspective toward arts and music, characterized by Chinese culture scholar Joseph Leveson as an "amateur ideal," helps to explain why most literati preferred to involve themselves in the arts and music but viewed themselves as amateurs even though their skills were not necessarily "amateurish." This attitude stands in stark contrast to the idea of music professionalism in most contemporary Western societies, where at least professional musicians enjoy high cultural status despite their relatively low social status. The exception is found in "star" performers who are respected by and associated with upper-class culture.

ACTIVITY 1.6 *Now that you understand how the terms* amateur *and* amateurish *were used in traditional China, reflect on how you use these words in your own environment. Which musicians and music-making do you know for whom these terms seem appropriate? Based on your own experience and observation, write a definition of* professional *versus* amateur.

The long tradition of music scholarship in China was continuously shaped by the dominant Confucian ideology and its social stratification. The goal of many music scholars who adhered to the Confucian ideology of music was to avoid practical musical matters and focus instead on abstract writing about music's relationship to cosmology and ethics. The elite buttressed its position in the social hierarchy by propagating its own values and cultural practices while disparaging those of subordinate groups, including the practicing musicians.

The relationship between the elite and professional musicians was a delicate one because *yiren* or *minjian yiren* were often needed to perform in social rites for the elite. Although granted a low social status, *minjian yiren* were essential for maintaining and preserving the literati's musical ideal that treated music as an attainment of spirituality and an accompaniment to various religious ritual and social ceremonies such as weddings and funerals. By not actually participating in the music-making on such occasions, members of the literati class were able to maintain their respected social positions and distance while at the same time enjoying music produced by those whom they considered inferior.

The Confucian classification of musicians, however, does not apply to the post-1949 situation. The communist transformation of the society altered the status of musicians and musical practice. Since 1949, the government has created a class of professional musicians as part of its propaganda team by employing a large number of formerly low-class *minjian yiren*. These musicians, now called *zhuanye* (professional or specialist) musicians, were selected partially because they were of their nonelite class background. However, many former elite musicians were excluded from this new classification and redefined as amateur musicians. This policy inadvertently produced a new definition for "amateur" musicians whose social status is the opposite of that in the earlier period. During my fieldwork, I had the opportunity of talking to a large number of *zhuanye* professional musicians who spoke disparagingly about "amateur" musicians and their musical practice.

At present, being amateur no longer carries the prestige once enjoyed by the literati. "Amateur" has been turned into a code word for someone who is not hired by the government, is untrained, and lacks formal musical knowledge. They are often looked down at by government *zhuanye* musicians. Ironically, some "amateur" musicians are excellent musicians in their own right even though they received little or no training. In fact, amateur music clubs sponsored by local government district offices are flourishing in many urban and rural areas, specifically after the death of Mao in 1976 and since the 1980s. This clearly indicates that apart from government-employed *zhuanye* musicians, a tremendous number of musicians are not employed as full-time professional musicians but nonetheless are actively engaging in various music activities. Because of the unique social context, the former professional-amateur dichotomy has shifted and the classification of musicians has been transformed.

The drastic sociopolitical transformation that has taken place since 1949 has undermined the traditional social-cultural system that distinguished between the group of people who made music and the function that music-making fulfilled. According to Mao's cultural policy, the primary function of the arts is to serve the needs of workers, peasants, and soldiers. The elite, mostly educated urban writers and artists who were familiar with both Chinese and Western ideas had to abandon their traditional aesthetic bias, embrace the current ideology, and produce works in line with the political climate that would appeal to what the government referred to as "the masses." Elite culture and upper-class music of the pre-1949 period were viewed as dangerous; thus they were unacceptable and needed to be discontinued in the new society.

For the communist government, musical activities became an effective tool by which the state could disseminate its ideological discourse. Through cultural productions, such as *yangge* (field song) and *wenyi wanhui* (evening cultural show), music and performing arts were successfully integrated with politics. Many traditional *minjian* musical activities that had been of low cultural status and customarily associated with various kinds of social rites, festivals, and local entertainment became legitimized as the heritage of the masses to be treasured and promoted by the communist government after the 1950s. Lu Ji, an important figure in the official musical establishment, set the tone and direction for music workers in his 1953 address to the National Musicians' Association, urging members to focus on developing amateur musical activities. The traditional terminology of *minjian yiren* (local or regional performing artists), which had indexed low social class in the prerevolutionary period, began to acquire a positive connotation. Many regional performing artists and their traditions came to be considered emblematic of the communist ideology because they were seen as representative of the masses and therefore politically significant.

The success story of the blind street *erhu* player Abing is a point in case (see chapter 2). Although he was discovered by the music scholar Yang Yinliu prior to 1949, Abing has been regarded as a cultural hero in the post-1949 period not only because of his musical achievement but also because his class background manifests populist ideology.

In the same vein, a considerable amount of scholarly effort was mobilized to preserve, disseminate, and document those local traditions that entail "correct" political elements. It is under such circumstances in the early years after the 1949 revolution that a number of regional instrumentalists emerged as key professional performers. Most of them were invited to perform in various state-sponsored public concerts and variety shows in the capital as well as other major provincial cities throughout the 1950s. With the support of the state, these performers soon became prominent teachers and famous professional musicians in state music institutions.

Since the communist government took power in 1949, government music institutions such as Minyuetuan (Traditional Music Orchestra), Gewutuan (Song and Dance Troupe), art academies, and music conservatories have been established with the primary function of cultivating a music that reflects the dominant sociopolitical ideology. In alignment with government ideals of development (*fazhan*) and being scientific (*kexuehua*), a musical language that combines selected Western and regional music elements has gradually taken shape and has emerged as the musical lingua franca for all genres of *minyue* or traditional national music. This homogenized pan-Chinese musical style was quickly adopted by government performing troupes across the nation and disseminated through public concerts, recordings, and the mass media. Buttressed by a politically driven musical discourse, this modernized musical practice is now considered superior by many professional musicians, and the new musical ideal and aesthetics have influenced the way they view traditional regional music.

While I was beginning to grasp the nature of amateur music practice, my teachers at the conservatory kept reminding me that the music of the teahouses and parks was only for fun and that it was unscientific and lacked specificities and organization in contrast to the music cultivated by professional musicians in the last fifty years. Their disparaging comments about *minjian* folk music revealed a bias commonly held by most professional musicians in China. So where does this place the music of amateurs and their regional traditions in the concept of "Chinese music"?

MUSIC REGIONALISM AND THE MEANING OF REGIONAL MUSIC

China is a big country, and any meaningful discussion of its music requires one to consider music from different regions. In one sense, Chinese music is made up of many regional genres, and one usually needs to identify the region from which a music originates. In similar vein, a person's identity is invariably defined in terms of place of origin or ancestral homeland and social class. Regardless of where one lives, the sense of identification with the place of one's origin (*jiguan*) and not one's birthplace is an important notion that grounds an individual. This tie to a specific region is manifested in multiple ways such as dialects, cultural practice, food, and music. Together, these cultural practices become emblems of a regional identity. However, in the modern context, regional music is often used as one of the necessary ingredients that make up what is generally called Chinese music, a collective category that is tied to the emergence of modern nationalism. This view also redefines Chinese music and the place of regional music vis-à-vis a collective label called national music. I will return to this in chapter 2.

Under the new definition of "Chinese music," regional music, *difang yinyue,* takes on two somewhat unfavorable meanings. First, regional music traditions are viewed as building blocks whose significance only lies in their contribution to shaping the overall characteristics of elite musical genres. Many Chinese scholars view them as parts of a large musical system rather than as traditions that have their musical merits and separate identities. Consequently, rather than seeing regional musical differences in their own terms and as products of their environment, the scholars often view them as subsets or parts of the stylistic core and practice. As a case in point, the scholar Ye Dong (1983) draws on different regional wind and percussion *chuida* traditions (chapter 3) to illustrate the stylistic origin of the genre of *chuida,* thus focusing on the unifying features rather than on differences among various regional traditions. Similarly, scholars Li and Yuan (1987), among others, emphasize the significant stylistic contributions of regional practice and the way they shape the individual solo instrumental traditions, such as those of Chaozhou *guzheng* (chapter 2), Shandong *suona,* northern *dizi* (chapter 2), or Jiangnan *pipa* (chapter 2).

The second view regards regional music as raw material and as music of the "other." It is common for most composers and scholars to view regional musics as ingredients that can be added as spice to enhance the flavor of new compositions—exemplifying the cultural elitist attitude of many nineteenth century European musicians' involvement in musical nationalism.

A third way of looking at *difang yinyue* is more positive. Using a concept similar to the German romanticists' notion of *volksmusik* (folk music), many contemporary Chinese composers hold that regional music, despite its "crude" and "unsophisticated" quality, embodies the true spirit of the people. They also believe that it is only through the process of refinement and development that the essence of this music can be brought out. This presentation has given rise to the practice of incorporating elements of regional music in original compositions. The fact that many composition students at the conservatories are often required to conduct field research to collect raw material for their compositions is a telling result of such an attitude (Yang 1994).

These three views have dominated the recent discourse on Chinese music and have redefined the meaning of regional music. In textbooks and music dictionaries, the portrayal of Chaozhou music, for instance, inevitably reflects this sentiment. Although Chaozhou music is known to have consisted of several unique instrumental genres, most descriptions of this music focus only on one or two genres. These genres are often mentioned when discussing other musical genres or are simply cited as examples of a regional deviation from the norm. Yuan Jingfang, a prominent music scholar on instrumental music, mentioned Chaozhou *zheng* repertory merely in passing when discussing solo *zheng* music but without providing an overall account of Chaozhou music (Yuan 1987). Others scholars also approach Chaozhou music from a similar perspective and tacitly downplay the overall uniqueness of Chaozhou music. A glance through the catalog of state-run China Records also reveals this bias. The number of recorded modern compositions based on Chaozhou musical elements is almost as plentiful as the recordings of traditional pieces. This preference clearly indicates that compositions that have incorporated Chaozhou musical stylistic features are treated as equal to, if not better than, the original repertories. In short, the image of Chaozhou music traditions as regional variants with exotic color underlies most discussions of this music.

This chapter has set the stage for the exploration of Chinese music. I began by describing the vivid life of regional music in different parts of China and introducing the concepts of amateur versus professional musicians. These discussions provide channels through which to understand contemporary musical life, music institutions, and the status of musicians, all of which are helpful for grasping the complexity of the Chinese musical system. This approach has hopefully prepared you to tackle these questions: What is Chinese music? What are the criteria for defining Chinese music? Who are the musicians, and how are they trained? Obviously there is no single answer to these questions, and it is only through an examination of various dimensions of Chinese music that these questions can be properly addressed. I will begin the next chapter by discussing the question of national music.

Constructing National Music

DEFINING "NATIONAL MUSIC" (*GUOYUE*)

In many countries, an intensification of nationalistic sentiments and pride has inspired the creation of national culture and practices. The rise of China's national music *guoyue* is no exception. Also known as *minzu yinyue* or abbreviated as *minyue, guoyue*—literally, "music of the nation"—is perceived first and foremost as different from any kind of imported music. But what is considered *guoyue* by Chinese musicians has not remained the same, and its meaning has gone through transformations corresponding to specific social and ideological underpinnings of historical periods alongside the changing concept of China as a country or nation (Figure 1.2).

According to Chinese music scholar Yu Siuwah, the term *guoyue* first appeared in the mid-fourteenth-century *Music Record of the History of Liao Dynasty* (907–1125). There, it was used to differentiate between music of the Khitan ruling class and that of the subjugated Han Chinese (Yu 1996: 119–136). During the Qing dynasty (1644–1911), its meaning changed and the term was used to refer to a kind of ceremonial court repertoire that came to function as a de facto "representation of China." Since the founding of the Republic government in the early twentieth century, musicians have adopted the label *guoyue* loosely to include all music written for Chinese instruments. This definition of *guoyue* was formulated in response to a particular nationalistic consciousness, following China's repeated defeats in wars with other countries. The term was used not only to differentiate Chinese music from foreign music but also symbolically to align music with the nation-building project. At the same time, the definition of Chinese music was restricted to music of the Han majority, the largest ethnic group in China. Over 95 percent of Chinese are of Han origin. Acknowledging the fact there are many ethnic groups residing within China, the Republic government designated the Han, Manchu, Mongolian, Hui, and Tibetan people as the primary ethnic groups of the Chinese nation. Since 1949, the

PRC government amended this schema and officially defines China as a multiethnic country with fifty-six recognized "nationalities," including the Han and others.

Despite prevalent use of the term *guoyue* in the early twentieth century, not all Chinese musicians agreed on its definition. At best, they agreed that *guoyue* was not Western music, known as *xiyue* or *yangyue,* which at that time meant Western military music, Christian hymns, and schools songs imported by way of Japan. To understand how China created its own national music, a brief account of how indigenous musicians confronted the arrival of Western culture is in order.

European music was brought to China through the military, missionaries, merchants, and Western travelers especially since the late nineteenth century. It was valorized and respected by local Chinese musicians because they equated Western music with the supremacy of Western science and technology. Against this cultural backdrop, Chinese music was considered by local musicians as unscientific and backward. Learning Western music came not only as a fad but also as a way to embrace the concept of being modern and to redefine one's social status. Western music's popularity with the general public soared as strophic songs with simple chord accompaniments were taught in schools. Because of this emphasis, the gap between Western and Chinese music widened. Many Chinese were drawn to European music, resulting in an increasing number of Chinese musicians practicing European classical music.

All agreed that China should have its own national music, but opinion varied as to what that should be. To resist the adoption of Western music, some traditionalists proposed a new Chinese national music by restructuring the practice of traditional Chinese music using only Chinese instruments. Others were in favor of using European music and instruments as the foundation of a new national music. Students who studied in Japan and later in Europe and the United States were particularly keen on putting their musical knowledge into practice, resulting in the establishment of new music institutions and a concert culture based on those of Western nations. At the same time, publications bearing the label *guoyue,* national music, began to appear in music books and collections as market demands for these books soared. Figure 2.1 is taken from a music collection published in the 1930s with the word *guoyue,* "national music," prominently displayed on the front cover.

As one can see, the debates between the traditionalists and modernists were as much a debate over musical taste and preference as they were related to the crisis confronting China's own cultural identity and

FIGURE 2.1   *Cover of a 1930s music publication bearing the name* Guoyue. *(Courtesy of Frederick Lau)*

the strategies for modernizing the country. For traditionalists, *guoyue* could only mean the music of Confucian rituals and the music of the literati, not regional or folk genres. The more open-minded extended the term to include all regional instrumental music, opera, and solo pieces as long as the music was not European. Several prominent Cantonese musicians also referred to Cantonese music as *guoyue* while many regional music clubs also called their music *guoyue*. The work of the educator Liu Tianhua at the Peking University [*sic*] in the 1920s is a good example of how Chinese regional music was incorporated into modern education institutions. Another example is the adoption of Peking opera as national music. Peking opera, once a regional opera, had acquired a reputation as *guoju* "national opera" because of the centrality of Peking as the political and cultural center of China. Its opera and dialect were considered to contain the essence of national culture.

Following the establishment of the PRC government in 1949 and the relocation of the Republic government to Taiwan, an officially sponsored national music finally emerged. Buttressed by communist ideology and an anticapitalist stance, the PRC government was eager to construct a national culture in order to reflect its proletarian ideology and to serve the majority of peasants, soldiers, and workers. To reach this objective, reforms were carried out in all aspects of society. In music, the reform directly affected music institutions, performance, aesthetics, status of musicians (chapter 1), and research agenda. In this new conception of *guoyue*, the term was changed to *minzu yinyue* ("national or people's music"), or its abbreviation, *minyue*, in order to reflect the communist populist ideology (see chapter 3).

Today, *minzu yinyue* is an encompassing category that includes all compositions and genres for traditional instruments. While the music is traditional in sound production, many musical pieces are newly composed and have incorporated new aesthetic ideals and performance practice. Chinese national music in the late twentieth century—Chinese "people's music"—encompasses multiple characteristics and includes many genres, such as Chinese orchestral music, regional music, vocal music, and solo repertory.

In the Republic of China (Taiwan), *guoyue* has continued on trajectories established by the Republicans according to their political vision of the nation. By emphasizing Chinese mainland culture over local Taiwanese culture, the Republic government hoped to establish its political legitimacy by promoting many Chinese musical genres, which they brought to Taiwan after 1949. Nancy Guy's 2005 monograph is an informative study that describes the process through which the Taiwanese government manipulates the perpetuation of *jingju* in Taiwan. However, the emergence of an indigenous Taiwanese identity and politics in the mid-1990s ultimately led the government to withdraw its support for many *jingju* troupes and training schools in the island. In view of the developments in the last century in the PRC and Republic of China, the definition of Chinese music cannot be assumed to be a single, centralized, and monolithic style. To do so would be misleading and overtly confining. Given the ongoing contributions of the conservatories, the musicians' active musical involvement and initiatives, and colorful regional music, an understanding of Chinese national music requires us to take them into consideration regardless of preference, styles, and history. Despite political differences between the PRC and Taiwan, *guoyue* on both sides of the straits has become quite similar in recent years because of cultural exchanges between the two governments since the 1990s. Regional traditions, stage performance, and formalized performance practice and training have become trademarks of national music in both places regardless of political allegiances.

Brief history of the Republic of China. *Dynasty China ended its two thousand years of history in 1911 when the Kuomingtang (KMT, Chinese Nationalists Party) led by Sun Yat-sen successfully overthrew the Qing dynasty and established the first Republic government in China. Sun Yat-sen was the first elected president of the Republic. Sun's untimely death in 1925 opened an opportunity for Chiang Kai Shek to lead the KMT. From 1927 to 1945, China was plagued by struggle among the KMT, CCP, foreign invasion, and warlords. It was during a 1927 internal struggle between the CCP and KMT that Chiang established his own national government in Nanjing in 1927. The subsequent expulsion of the CCP from KMT marked the beginning of the Chinese Civil War. It lasted until 1945 when Chiang's KMT government was defeated and relocated to Taiwan.*

To ensure the dissemination of *guoyue* and its centrality in the PRC society, new music institutions were necessary. The following section examines the rise of conservatories in the twentieth century and their role in cultivating a new national music for the nation.

INSTITUTIONS AND THE NATIONAL MUSIC CONSERVATORY

The adoption of Western-style education in schools in the early twentieth century changed how music was taught. Whereas traditional musical training in China was done largely between a teacher and student utilizing methods of rote playing and oral transmission, there was no standardized pedagogical and repertory among teachers across the nation. Many missionary schools provided music training, especially in piano, music theory, and singing, changing the study of music into a legitimate subject of study and also a tool for the cultivation of morality and individuality in the modern age. With the formation of performance groups and educational organizations such as the Shanghai Municipal Orchestra in 1879, the Shanghai Orphanage Orchestra in 1908, and the Shanghai College Music Department in 1906, training of China's musicians on Western instruments gained momentum as China embarked on its modernization project.

Conservatory training in China started with the founding of the National Music Conservatory (later the Shanghai Conservatory of Music) in 1927. Founded by two Western-trained educators, Cai Yuanpei (who studied at the Universität Leipzig and was the first president of Peking University) and Xiao Yaomei (who trained in Japan and Germany), the conservatory was to promote national music by incorporating and utilizing Chinese and European music as its mission. The initial curriculum was limited to theory and composition, piano, symphonic strings and winds, vocal music, and Chinese music. The implementation of a formalized curriculum and pedagogy signified the beginning of modern music education in China. Since its establishment, it has become the leading institution for Western music training in China and a model for many universities and college music programs. The National Music Conservatory was responsible for producing many of the first generation of Chinese musicians of European classical music.

For Chinese music, the conservatory developed a systematic way of teaching traditional music and codified its playing style and performance practice for all instruments. Modeled on the Western practice of instrumental solos, it also created a canon of solo pieces for every instrument, including those that had traditionally been played only in ensembles. A national standard for all music training was put in place soon after 1949 when the government centralized all music academies and conservatories. The conservatory's name was officially changed to the Shanghai Conservatory of Music, and several major conservatories were also set up across the country under the supervision of the Ministry of Culture of the PRC.

The shift from a traditional training method to formal conservatory training in the post-1949 period inevitably affected the social status of musicians. As discussed in chapter 1, a new generation of trained musicians was esteemed as new cultural elite rather than disparaged as low class as in traditional China. Because of the cultural prestige placed on their conservatory training and their qualifications as graduates of the conservatories, trained musicians became respected and seen as professional (*zhuanye*) musicians and specialists. The conservatory thus has become a desirable place of higher education producing highly qualified performing musicians and composers. Most graduates are now receiving a sizable salary and a secure career in teaching and performing music.

At present, there are eight major national conservatories and numerous provincial music academies across the country. All offer general musical training, and some offer comprehensive degree programs in both Western and traditional Chinese music.

With the emergence of music conservatories, the configuration of post-1949 national music took on a direction different from that of the previous era. The following section focuses on the two most prominent components of the new *guoyue* in the late twentieth century: the Chinese orchestra and solo practices.

THE CHINESE ORCHESTRA

The Chinese orchestra was another significant force in the creation of Chinese national music. The Chinese orchestra is a twentieth-century invention (Figure 2.2). Modeled on the structure of a Western symphonic orchestra, its instrumentation and repertory have been standardized in the last several decades, a process that began in the 1930s. Nowadays, Chinese orchestras are a cultural icon that can be found in almost every major city across the country and in places where there is a sizable Chinese population, such as Hong Kong, Taiwan, Singapore, Malaysia, Toronto, and Los Angeles.

Ensembles of mixed strings and winds have existed throughout Chinese music history. They were used in court rituals or during large-scale religious ceremonies. For example, in ancestral worship or Confucian rituals, sixty-four-piece orchestras of winds, strings, and percussion instruments, usually in formation, would perform ritual music outside the shrine. Sometimes foreign instruments would be mixed in with indigenous instruments, as in the Tang dynasty ensemble *Shibuji* (Ten orchestras) and Ming dynasty *Siyiwu* (Barbarian dance).

Small ensembles performing popular music began to emerge during the eleventh to twelfth centuries. Soon, this type of mixed ensemble was adopted in folk traditions and secular entertainment music. The preference for small ensembles and vocal genres eventually overshadowed other types of ensembles and confined large ensembles to court ceremonies and large-scale clan-based rituals such as ancestral worship.

The brief history of the modern Chinese orchestra began by the expansion of the small *jiangnan sizhu* ensemble. In the late 1920s,

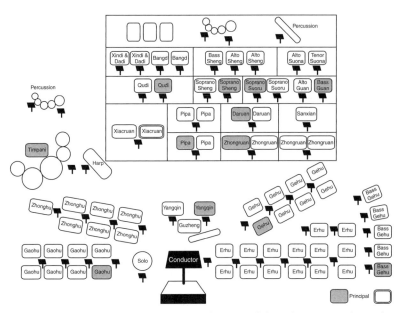

FIGURE 2.2 *Modern chinese orchestra. The setup of the orchestra is similar to that of a European symphonic orchestra, with strings in the front, winds and percussion in the back. The conductor stands on a podium to the center and front of the orchestra. (Courtesy of Frederick Lau)*

Shanghai-based musician Zheng Zhiwen began to experiment with his new compositional strategy by increasing the number of the *jiangnan sizhu* ensemble up to thirty-five players. By increasing the size of each section and combining different instruments, Zheng inadvertently established a model on which the modern Chinese orchestra was based. In his experimentation, he separated the strings and winds into sections and further subdivided the former into bowed and plucked strings. To increase the volume and density of the ensemble, he added additional players to each section. In terms of the music, Zheng relinquished the traditional practice of individual players embellishing the parts at will and began to compose specific music for each instrument or section, thus shifting the control of the music from performers to composers. Although Zheng's model did not attract much attention during his time, his vision of large ensemble and musical innovation has been influential in the formation of the modern Chinese orchestra.

In terms of organization, a Chinese orchestra is slightly different from the Western symphony orchestra. A Chinese orchestra is made up of four groups of instruments: bowed strings, plucked strings, winds, and percussion (Figure 2.2). The largest section is the bowed strings that include various sizes of bowed lutes such as *erhu*, the high-pitched *gaohu* (tuned a fourth higher than the *erhu*), the medium-range *zhonghu*, and the cellolike low-pitched *gehu*. The plucked strings section consists of plucked lutes and plucked and hammered zithers that include the *pipa, liuyeqin, zhongruan, daruan, sanxian, guzheng,* and hammered dulcimer *yangqin*. More than any other instruments, the use of plucked and hammered strings is what gives the orchestra its unique tone and color. The wind section is made up of a combination of flutes and reed instruments. The most prominent winds (aerophones) are the different sizes of the side-blown flute *dizi* (Figure 1.9) and the vertical flute *xiao* (Figure 1.10), which are used interchangeably. The reed instruments are the mouth organ *sheng* (Figure 1.11) and the double-reed *suona* (Figure 1.12). All these instruments produce a nasal and piercing tone without Western counterparts. The last group is the percussion section. Figure 1.13 shows a set of commonly used Chinese percussions in a village setting. This collection of idiophones and membranophones is also being adopted in the Chinese orchestra. The instruments include the double-headed Chinese drums *dagu* (a single big drum) and *paigu* (a set of several drums), big cymbals *dabo*, handheld *naobo*, handheld gong *luo*, frame-mounted tam-tams consisting of ten small tam-tams mounted on a special frame called a *shi mian luo*, bell *ling* (a bell tree consisting of five suspended bells *ma ling*), woodblocks of various sizes, and timpani.

ACTIVITY 2.1 *Focus on a few websites about the Chinese orchestra with good graphics and prepare answers to these questions:*

1. *What is the seating arrangement of the orchestra? That is, where do the players of the different instrument sit—in sections or intermingled? Of the former, do you see sections arranged into the same seating pattern from orchestra to orchestra?*

2. *How many players of each instrument do you find, and do you find similar proportions of instrument type from orchestra to orchestra?*

3. *Find a website for or consult a friend a teacher about the lay-out of a European orchestra and compare this with the Chinese orchestras.*

4. *Listen to the Chinese orchestral piece on CD track 14 and then the* jiangnan sizhu *except on CD track 1. Write a comparison between the two pieces by focusing on the texture, timbre, orches-tration, dynamics, and treatment of the main melody. In your own words, what makes the Chinese orchestral music different from the* jiangnan sizhu?

During the 1950s and 1960s, the government's systematic approach to revamping traditional music sparked new interests in further transforming traditional ensembles into orchestras. The first post-1949 Chinese orchestra was established in 1953 as the Central Broadcasting Station Orchestra in Beijing. In addition to adopting the model estab-lished by Zheng earlier, tuning of the instruments has been shifted to the equal-tempered tuning system, much like that of the piano. Many instruments were added to enhance the sound quality and range of the orchestra. Many of its compositions were arrangements of regional ensemble music reorchestrated for a large ensemble. A large number of the early compositions were based on traditional wind and percussion pieces. Lyrical pieces, compositions with themes derived from or asso-ciated with national minorities, and instrumental solos with orchestral accompaniment were gradually added to the repertory.

As it is used today, the modern Chinese orchestra is similar to the Western symphony orchestra in terms of performance practice, sonic ideals, and compositional strategy. However, in just several decades, the Chinese orchestra has become one of the most effective institutions in changing the development of Chinese music from mostly heterophonic music to polyphonic and homophonic music. There is a tendency to write for orchestras with unusually large groups of instruments and techni-cally challenging passages. Composers are also interested in exploring new terrain of new instrumental solos with orchestra. Some even discard the traditional Chinese-sounding scales in favor of experimenting with atonal music and avant-garde style. Among the many changes that have occurred in Chinese music, the Chinese orchestra continues to grow and offer much room for composers to express their creative impulses.

The Chinese Orchestra in Hong Kong. The modern Chinese orchestra has become an important cultural institution inside and outside China despite its relatively short history. In many overseas Chinese communities, it has been viewed as an emblem of Chinese culture. It is easy to find a Chinese orchestra in large Chinese communities such as those in Taiwan, Singapore, and Malaysia as well as cities such as Hong Kong, Toronto, Malaysia, Vancouver, and San Francisco. Focusing on the situation in Hong Kong, I show how a complex Chinese identity emerged with the influence of the British colonial government and at present under the Hong Kong government since the 1997 return of Hong Kong to the PRC.

The Hong Kong Chinese Orchestra (HKCO, Figure 2.3) was founded in 1977 by the former urban council of the local Hong Kong government. The colonial government attempted to neutralize anticolonial sentiments that surfaced in late 1960s by promoting Chinese culture. The HKCO was supported financially by the government's Leisure and Cultural Services. As the only professional Chinese orchestra in Hong Kong, the orchestra has assumed the important task of promoting modern Chinese music. However, Hong Kong's eclectic cultural background and colonial past have shaped the development of Chinese

FIGURE 2.3 *Hong Kong Chinese Orchestra. (Courtesy of Frederick Lau)*

music in special ways. In April 2001, HKCO became an independent agency that is not under the direct sponsorship of the government.

Although the structure and performance practice of the HKCO are similar to those in the PRC, its repertory is unique and includes traditional, contemporary, and popular pieces. To maintain its own identity, HKCO promotes works by contemporary local Hong Kong composers and Chinese composers around the world. Since its inception, the orchestra has commissioned more than fifteen hundred new works. In 2002, the orchestra was awarded "the most outstanding achievement in advancing contemporary Chinese music" by the International Society of Contemporary music (a worldwide organization based in Europe).

Other kinds of innovation are part of the orchestra's mission. Since 1998, it has presented concerts with special themes such as *Chinese Music Select, Music from the Heart, Valentine Day's Concert, Composers Series,* and *Fascinating Conductors* as well as additional concerts of regional music and instrumental ensemble music. In 1998, it set a new Guinness Record by having over one thousand *erhu* players at a group performance entitled *Music from a Thousand Strings.* To further popularize Chinese music, the orchestra is actively engaging in educational programs and instrument classes. In 2002, it presented a concert of the most popular Chinese works of the twentieth century to introduce the standard orchestral repertory to its audience. Glancing at the programming of the orchestra, one can sense that here the notion of Chineseness takes on a cosmopolitan flavor and a sense of worldliness rather than being narrowly defined according to a regional or localized identity.

SOLO REPERTORY IN THE MAKING

Another major development in the new *minzu yinyue* ("people's music") was the creation of solo repertory. Demand for solo pieces increased as the performance of traditional music was moved to the concert stage from informal settings. While there had long been solo traditions for instruments such as the *pipa* (Figure 1.5, CD track 4), *guqin* (Figure 2.4, CD track 37), and *erhu* (Figure 1.4, CD track 2), musicians began to compose solo pieces for all traditional instruments. Under the post-1949 central government's new music policy, solo traditions for all instruments flourished. The basis of these pieces came from two sources: arrangements of ensemble music for one instrument and transcriptions of pieces originally written for other instruments with the addition of new accompaniments.

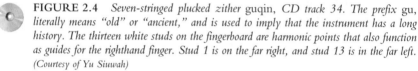

FIGURE 2.4 *Seven-stringed plucked zither* guqin, *CD track 34. The prefix* gu, *literally means "old" or "ancient," and is used to imply that the instrument has a long history. The thirteen white studs on the fingerboard are harmonic points that also function as guides for the righthand finger. Stud 1 is on the far right, and stud 13 is in the far left. (Courtesy of Yu Siuwah)*

Solo Repertory for Dizi.　*Dizi* is a wind instrument popular in many regional genres across the country (Figure 1.9, CD track 8). This indigenous side-blown bamboo flute has a long and documented history. Contrary to its current history and popularity, *dizi* music was relatively obscure prior to 1949, and not much music from ancient times has survived to the present. Part of the reason for this was the low status of both the players and the instrument. However, perceptions of *dizi* music have undergone drastic change since the Communist Revolution in 1949. The most important development has been the intense government involvement in regulating and standardizing its music. Before the 1950s, the term *dizi music* referred loosely to any music that could be played on a *dizi* rather than to a specific body of literature. Since 1949, under the close supervision of the government and the establishment of government-sponsored music conservatories throughout the nation, this *dizi* music, along with that for many other traditional instruments, has been systematically developed to serve the ideological needs of the communist regime in representing the common folk. With the institutionalizing of music and the establishing of conservatories and professional performing troupes, the idea of *dizi* solo with a standardized performance practice and repertory was established.

　　The development of *dizi* music from 1949 up to the late 1980s can be roughly divided into three periods, each characterized by a unique style of composition (Lau 1991). In the first period (1949–1964), most compositions were derived directly from a number of regional ensemble pieces such as those from the northern *errentai*—a song-and-dance genre from the Shaanxi and Inner Mongolia region—and the southern *jiangnan sizhu*—the silk and bamboo tradition from the Shanghai region (CD track 1). During this period pieces were created simply by extracting the original melody and adding a number of variations. This method of composing became a standard model for many solo *dizi* pieces in this period.

In the second period (1964–1976) came a decline in relying on the once popular theme-and-variation procedure and an increased use of varied source materials as a basis for compositions. These musical sources included revolutionary mass songs (see chapter 5), fragments of traditional melodies, and sometimes original compositions written in the traditional idiom. Perhaps the most significant development was the use of a traditional orchestra as accompaniment and the standardization of form of *dizi* compositions. *Dizi* composers adopted a formulaic three-part form—either slow-fast-slow or vice versa, and they often open with a cadenzalike solo passage in the introduction.

Unfortunately, the third period—the ten years of the political struggle called the Cultural Revolution (1966–1976)—put a damper on any further development. The Cultural Revolution was the result of a struggle for power between Mao and his enemies. As a way to continue the spirit of revolution and to prevent China from regressing into a traditional elitist society, Mao organized the urban youths into Red Guards and encouraged them to attack all traditional values and bourgeois behavior and ideology. It started in Beijing but quickly spread to other parts of the country. Consequently, many traditional cultural artifacts, including books, art objects, and historical buildings, were destroyed. Most Western and traditional Chinese music and instruments were banned except for the officially endorsed "model opera" (see chapter 5). It was not until after the fall of the Gang of Four and the death of Mao in 1976 that many *dizi* composers resumed their activities. The Gang of Four was a group of radical politicians headed by Chairman Mao Zedong's wife Jiang Qing. Their goal was to return China to a political freneticism focused on the cult of Mao.

The most essential techniques in contemporary *dizi* playing can be classified into two distinct schools according to its place of origin, namely the southern *nanpai* (CD track 15) and northern *beipai* (CD track 16). The features of these two styles are founded on an approach toward tone production that includes methods of embellishing and ornamenting the melody.

The southern school refers to a style of lyrical playing similar to that found in classical opera *kunqu* (CD track 17) and *jiangnan sizhu* (CD track 1). The *qudi* (*dizi* used in *kunqu* opera), because of its mellow tone quality, is often used in this southern style of playing. Music written in this style is usually slow and expressive. The ornaments are predominantly simple short melodic turns, trills, and appoggiatura (fast notes played before the main note).

ACTIVITY 2.2   *Listen to the southern style on CD track 15 and describe the stylistic features of the piece and playing techniques. From the description given in the text, compare what you hear in this example to the example of* jiangnan sizhu *on CD track 1. How are they different? Do they have similar sonic features? If so, what are they?*

The northern school, on the contrary, is characterized by a fast and rhythmic playing often accompanied by a brilliant and shrill tone quality (CD track 16). The *dizi* used in the northern style is a shorter instrument, and it is usually higher in pitch and more piercing in tone quality than the *dizi* used in the southern style. Music of the northern school is fast and virtuosic and accompanied by techniques such as glissando, tremolo, flutter tonguing, and fast tonguing. Although these techniques can be traced to a number of regional musical traditions, such as *jiangnan sizhu,* a northern song-and-dance genre called *errentai,* and *kunqu* and *bangzi* opera from northwest China, at present, they are adopted in compositions because of their unique sonic characters rather than to make reference to any specific geographical region.

The composer whose piece is featured on CD track 16 is Feng Zicun, a folk musician from northwestern China whose musical experience provides a good example. As a poor, itinerant musician, he grew up in the northern regional ensemble and instrumental tradition. Because of his skills, he was invited by the post-1949 government to become a performer for the state's newly created music troupes. This invitation eventually transformed his life, and he was elevated to become a prominent performer because of his skills in the northern style. His career as a performer and composer soared in the newly implemented government music institution after he was discovered by the local cultural office. He performed in numerous concerts at home and abroad. His many recordings are representative examples of the northern style.

"Wubangzi" (CD track 16), a representative piece of the northern style, is often attributed to Feng as one of his "compositions." It is a standard northern solo based on a piece that originated from the Inner Mongolian region (Figure 1.2). It was later absorbed into the Shanxi province local opera and narrative as prelude and interlude. As for all performances of regional music, the performers were expected to elaborate on the melody by the same process I described for Chaozhou *xianshi* and Shanghai *jiangnan sizhu* music. Feng's "composition" is essentially a written-down version of his own playing. The piece is based on a theme stated in the beginning with four subsequent variations that elaborate the original melody. New notes and rhythm are added to the melody, thus changing the density of the piece. Characteristic techniques used in this piece include flutter tonguing and fast glissando in either upward or downward motion (Figure 2.5).

ACTIVITY 2.3 *Listen to the* dizi *piece "Wubangzi" on CD track 16 until you can easily follow the notation (Figure 2.5). Pay attention to the embellishments and the characteristics of the melody. Then photocopy the notation and put in the notation where you hear the embellishments and different techniques used throughout the piece. Try to describe what is different from variation to variation. In your own words, how is this piece different from the southern* dizi *style?*

Solo Repertory for **Erhu.** Perhaps the best known Chinese bowed chordophone, the *erhu* (Figure 1.4, CD track 2) is an important instrument in Chinese music. Also known as *huqin* ("barbarian lute"), the *erhu* was imported from Central Asia. The earliest documented history of the *huqin* appears during the tenth century; after that, this instrument and other regional variations of the *huqin* began to appear regularly in historical documents. Gradually it was absorbed into Chinese culture and became an indigenous Chinese instrument. Traditionally, the *erhu* was used as an ensemble instrument in regional traditions. Its mellow but slightly nasal tone quality and characteristic glissando have created an unmistakably sonic marker in Chinese music (see chapter 1).

During the twentieth century, it was shifted from being a folk instrument to an important solo instrument of the academy. The first person who was responsible for promoting *erhu* was Liu Tianhua (1895–1932). A trained Western music educator, Liu also had a strong

2/4   1=A   *Wubangzi*

Time

```
         fl            fl                    tr⌒
0:00  | 6·  7 |  6    5 |3̇  -- | 3   -- |5    -- |5   |i̇    tr⌒
         ⌒                                                6  1|2  --|2   --|
0:22  |3   5  |  5·  i̇ |  6   5 |  i̇   6 |  1  -- |1   -- |    2  5 |  7   2 |  6#5  6| 6  --|
                    fl                        fl      tr⌒              fl⌒
0:39  | 6   2   5 | 1·   2 | 7·  6 |  5    5   6 | 1·  7|6  1  6  1 |  3·5  6  1|5  -- |5  -- |
                                                              fl⌒
0:53  |5·3   5   6| 1  --|2  1̇ | 6·  1  6  5|3·5  2   3|5  -- |6   2|1  6|5  5  i̇|
                                 fl⌒
1:07  |3·  5   6  1|5  -- |5  -- |

1:12  | 6·  7  |  6   7  6  5|3̇   3  |3̇  3 |5·  0  5· 0|1·  0  3·  0|2̇  2|2̇  2|
1:22  |3·  0  5· 0| 5·  1  6  5|i̇ 1|i̇ 1|2   3  5|2  5  7  2|6  6|6  ·|
1:33  | 6   2   5 | 1·   2 | 7·  6|5  5  6 | 1   1  1|6  1  6  1|6  1  7  6|5  5  66|
1:41  |5 3  5|5·3  5  6| 1  --|2  1|6·  1  6  5|3·5  23|5  --|6  2̇|1  1  1  6|5  5  1|
1:51  |3·5  6  1|5  -- |5  --|

1:54  |6·  7|6  7   6  5|3  33|3  33|3  33|5  5  5  5|1  1  3  5|2  22  2  22|
2:00  |2  22  2  22|3  33  5  55|5  55  6  5|6161  6161|6161  6161|2  22  3  55|2  55|2  55|7  22|
```

2:06 | 6 77 | 6 77 | 6 77 | 6 77 | 6 66 2 5 | 1 1 1 6 | 5 5 5 6 | 1 1 1 1 | 6 1 6 1 | 6 1 6 1 |

2:12 | 5 1 5 1 | 5 1 | 5 1 | 5 11 5 6 | 1 -- | 2 1 | 6· 1 6 5 | 3 5 2 3 | 5 -- |

2:18 | 6 2 | 1 76 | 5 5 5 1 | 3·5 6 1 | 5 -- | 5 --- |

2:22 | 6 -- | 6 -- | 3 1 3 1 | 3 1 3 1 || 3 5 3 5 | 3 5 3 5 | 2 1 2 1 |

2:26 | 2 1 2 1 | 3 5 3 5 | 3 5 3 5 | 1 -- | 1 --- | 2 5 | 2 3 7 2 | 6 7 6 7 |

2:32 | 6 7 6 7 | 6 2 | 2 6 | 5 5 5 6 | 1 1 1 1 | 6 1 6 1 | 6 1 | 5 1 5 5 1 | 5 1 5 5 1 |

2:38 | 5 11 5 6 | 1 --- | 2 1 | 6·1 6 5 | 3 5 2 3 | 5·0 0 |

2:43 | 6 2 | 1 76 | 5 5 1 | 3·5 6 1 | 5 -- | 5 --- ||

Key: Fl - Flutter tongue
       Tr - Trill
        - glissando up
        - glissando down

FIGURE 2.5 *Notation of the dizi piece "Wubangzi" showing timings and sections, CD track 16.*

background in *kunqu* opera, *pipa,* and the regional music of Jiangsu province. Inspired by the anti-imperialist and patriotic fervor of the student-led protest called the May 4th Movement, Liu began to adopt Western music techniques and pedagogy for *erhu* playing as a way to modernize and promote Chinese music. Realizing that the *erhu* lacked a systematic training method similar to that of the violin, Liu wrote forty-seven *erhu* exercises to create a system. To promote his agenda, he also composed ten solos for the instrument. Liu's contribution was far-reaching. Not only did he establish the foundation of modern *erhu* playing, but he also elevated the instrument into the academy. At Peking University, he established the Guoyue Yanjiuhui (Association of National Music Research) and Guoyue Gaijinshe (National Music Improvement Society), two societies that were important in promoting Chinese music.

Blind Musician Abing (1893–1950).   Another musician who left an important mark on the history of *erhu* playing is Abing, a blind musician who became one of the most respected *erhu* players in communist China. Originally named Hua Yanjun (1893–1950), Abing was a Daoist monk who learned music from his father and was versatile in many *minjian* folk music genres. Daoism exists both as a philosophy and a religion. The philosophical view of Daoism advocates nonaggressive and natural ways of life. As a folk religion, Daoism is a form of mysticism that aims to control an esoteric way of accessing the sources of all cosmological processes or paths, called *dao.* Music is indispensable in Daoist ritual and the recitation of Daoist texts. Like many Daoist monks, Abing was an excellent musician who at age thirty-five lost his eyesight and became a street musician. His fortune turned when the musicologist Yang Yinliu (1899–1984) discovered him in 1950. Yang's in-depth study of Abing directly promoted Abing's reputation as a hero of the people and as a representation of the triumph of oppressed people in the new China. While studying Abing, Yang also recorded his performance. The recording on CD track 18 is an original recording of the piece "Moon at Second Spring" ("Erquan yingyue") performed by Abing.

This piece (CD track 18) has become one of the most performed pieces in the *erhu* solo repertory in recent years. The music purportedly depicts several aspects of Abing's life as a miserable poor and blind musician. The story goes something like this. Abing revisited his hometown and the Second Spring in Wuxi city. The Second Spring was reportedly designated by a Tang dynasty tea aficionado who traveled around China looking for the best springs to make tea. The best spring is located in a nearby town called Suzhou. While enjoying the tranquillity of this place, he was reminded of his humble background and poor life. A sense of familiarity and calm inspired him to renew his determination to live. Many scholars interpreted this story as Abing's appreciation of the new society where poor persons like himself were recognized and as a tacit commentary on feudal China.

"Erquan yingyue" has a simple structure. The main theme is made up of three short melodic segments (Figure 2.6a). The entire piece can be divided into six motivically related sections, and each section consists of variations of the three short melodic segments (Figure 2.6b). A detailed analysis of the sections reveals that the piece is constructed using the method of melodic expansion and diminution of the original melodic segments. Although the structure of the piece is not complicated, one can recognize when regional musicians usually utilize similar melodic material to create new compositions. Because of similar melodic material, there is a certain degree of coherence in the entire composition.

ACTIVITY 2.4 *Go to the Internet to investigate the Silk Road. What were "the Roads"? Who went where, when, and why? What part did China play? What did China send out and receive along "the Road"?*

Whether Abing's story has any basis in reality or not (this is a matter of scholarly disagreement), Abing is important in the development of *erhu* music. As a case in point, the study of Abing has become a popular topic of scholarly research and has figured prominently in recent Chinese music scholarship. British ethnomusicologist Jonathan Stock addresses the interests in Abing study and the controversy surrounding Abing's life story in his book *Musical Creativity in Twentieth-Century China: Abing, His Music, and Its Changing Meanings* (1996), where he examines questions like how Abing's narrative has been constructed and reflects on how various scholars have studied Abing's origin, life story, and social status. In questioning Yang Yinliu's account of Abing and his portrayal as a patriot and a revolutionary figure, Stock demystifies Abing's image and offers another approach through which to read music biography. He cautions us to be mindful that life stories can easily be created and imagined according to the writer's subjectivity and background. Studying Abing's story not only enlightens readers about the development of *erhu* music but also sheds light on the nuances in Chinese music historiography.

The three main melodic segments of "Erquan yingyue":

(a)
2· 3 1 12 | 3· 5 6 5 6561 | 5· 3 5 53 26 5612 | 3· 5 | 2·351 6235 | 1 -- etc.

(b)
1 61 3 23 | 1· 6 1·233 2 1·1 6123 | 5 - etc.

(c)
5035 6561 | 5·3 5 5 1 6 6 5655 | 3 5 3·#435 2·321 61 6 | 1· 2 351 2536 | 5 - etc.

Structure of "Erquan yingyue":

```
Introduction
Section 1:   a     b     c
Section 2:   a1    b     c1    c2
Section 3:   a1    a2    b     c1    c3    c4
Section 4:   a3    b1    c5    c6
Section 5:   a4    b1    c7    c8
Section 6:   a5    b1    c9
```

FIGURE 2.6 Structural analysis of "Erquan yingyue," CD track 18.

Solo Repertory for **Pipa.**   *Pipa* is a pear-shaped plucked lute with a history that dates back to the Han dynasty (202–220 C.E.) (Figure 1.5, CD track 4). Similar to the *huqin*, the *pipa* was imported from Central Asia along the Silk Road. In ancient times, there were two types of *pipa*, one with a straight neck and the other with a slightly bent neck. The older "bent"-neck *pipa* was believed to have been imported into China during the Jin dynasty (220–581 C.E.) from the Western part of China in modern-day Xinjiang and Gansu provinces (Figure 1.2).

ACTIVITY 2.5   *Go to the Internet and investigate the coun-tries that were covered along the Silk Road. Then compile a list of some of the treasures and everyday objects that were brought into China via the Silk Road.*

Prior to the Tang dynasty (618–907 C.E.), the *pipa* was used mainly in ensembles accompanying singing and dancing for the entertainment of the imperial and noble courts. It was during the Tang dynasty that the *pipa* began to be played as a solo instrument, both in and beyond the courts. The *pipa* also began to emerge as a major instrument in accompanying narrative singing such as *tanci* and opera such as *kunqu* and was an indispensable instrument in various instrumental ensembles. As with many instruments outside the literate tradition, the history of *pipa* music is sketchy. What we know about the *pipa* comes mostly from literary writings that tell us that the instrument was played by both the literati and musicians of low social status. In popular vernacular written documents, the *pipa* was depicted as an instrument of the courtesans and was used by female players who accompanied themselves while singing.

Today the *pipa* is known both as a solo and an ensemble instrument. According to scholar John Myers, the earliest known surviving *pipa* scores were published in the early nineteenth century. Discovered in the twentieth century, they were written in the tablature form from the late Tang and Five dynasties periods (618–959 C.E.). Because of the lite-rati's involvement, a major body of traditional pieces was preserved. However, from what little we know about the *pipa*, we can deduce that its music was mainly transmitted orally and that the scores were used mainly as aids to memory.

Four early collections of *pipa* music compiled by *pipa* performers in the nineteenth century are still used today. The names of these four collectors are Hua Qiuping (1784–1859), Li Fangyuan (b. c. 1850); Shen

Zhaozhou (1859–1930), and Shen Haochu (1889–1953). These collections were originally made as teaching or memory aids for the transmission of their own styles of playing. Needless to say, they offer significant clues to the understanding of the *pipa* repertory. Their music is notated in *gongche* notation, traditional Chinese notation that relies on numbers to represent pitches and dots and lines for rhythm (Figure 2.7). We can surmise that the score represents music passed down from an earlier period and that players were expected to embellish the melodies in performance.

In general, there are two types of titles in *pipa* pieces. One is non-programmatic, and the other is programmatic. Nonprogrammatic titles usually are abstract in nature, referring for instance to structure or number of beats or measures in a pieces such as "Liu ban" ("Six Beats") or

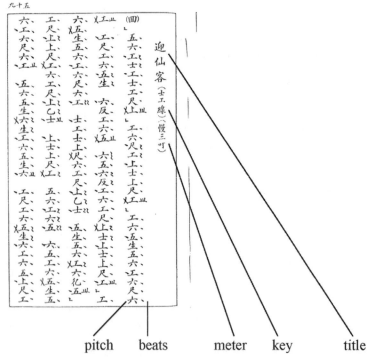

pitch   beats   meter   key   title

FIGURE 2.7 *Example of* gongche *notation. The notation is to be read from top to bottom and from right to left. (Courtesy of Frederick Lau)*

"Bantouqu" ("Piece Played before the Beat"). Pieces in the collections are programmatic; that is, they contain poetic titles that narrate stories or programs. The use of programmatic titles is an important feature in Chinese music. Programmatic music is music that narrates a story or refers to something concrete in reality, such as scenery, nature, a flowing stream, a flock of flying geese, and high mountains. It can also be poetic in tone and can depict historical events, human emotions, or states of mind.

Being both a literati and vernacular tradition, *pipa* music was often given more attention than that of other vernacular instruments. Its music was categorized according to different schemes, all of which were based on sets of binary oppositions. For instance, pieces that were based on length can be divided into *daqu* (large piece or suite) and *xiaoqu* (small piece). John Myers reports that there are more small pieces in the collections than there are large pieces. By definition, large pieces are longer and usually contain multiple sections. Most small pieces are shorter and have only one section. Both large and small pieces are further divided into civil (*wen*) and martial (*wu*) pieces. Civil pieces are often played at a slower tempo with a soft dynamic and subtle color. Since they are refined, elegant, and contemplative, they are considered feminine in nature. In contrast, *wu* pieces are more rhythmic, fast, loud, rigorous, and played with fast strumming and are considered masculine pieces. The concept of *wen* and *wu* is still applicable to other pieces as well and it is parallel with other binaries for describing music, as in *chu* (thick) and *xi* (refined), *nan* (south) and *bei* (north), or *yin* (restrained) and *yang* (expressive). These binaries offer the modern player a window through which to conceptualize these pieces.

Pipa music provides a rich source of information to explore the theme of musical regionalism in Chinese music. From these surviving scores, we can speculate that by the late nineteenth and early twentieth centuries, four schools of *pipa* playing were flourishing in the Jiangnan (lower Yangtze River valley) area, each named after the places where they had developed: Wuxi, Pinghu, Chongming, and Pudong, areas that are not too far from the city of Shanghai (Figure 2.8). The four printed *pipa* collections contain pieces and relevant information that marked the differences between the four schools. During the 1920s and 1930s, another school represented by Wang Yuting (1872–1951) in Shanghai took shape. The major differences among these schools were the different repertory as well as interpretations of the pieces.

Since the 1920s, intellectuals have played a role in the development of a *pipa* solo tradition, much like the evolution of music for the *erhu*.

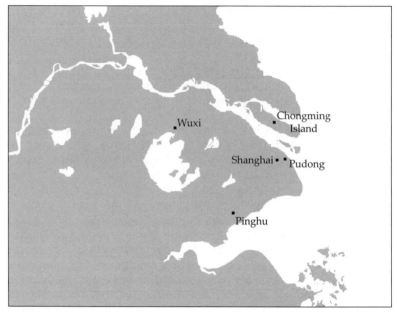

FIGURE 2.8 *Four important cities of* pipa *playing: Wuxi, Pinghu, Chongming, and Pudong.*

These players usually had some training in Western music, and, while familiar with traditional practice, they viewed Chinese instruments and music through Western frames. Liu Tianhua, the promoter of *erhu* music, was also an avid *pipa* player. Applying similar methods to improve the *pipa*, he proposed to make changes to the music using Western or cipher notation using Arabic numerals like that in Figure 2.5. He reconstructed the instrument by moving the frets of the *pipa* according to the twelve equal-tempered tuning. He also composed pieces for the *pipa*. His contributions to the *pipa* laid a firm foundation to the development of *pipa* as a solo instrument. Since the 1950s, the *pipa* solo has become a recognized solo genre in the *minyue* arena of "people's music" or national music.

CD track 19 is one of the most performed *pipa* solos in the repertory. "Shimian maifu" ("Ambush from All Directions") is a *wu* piece. The title is a literary reference to a fierce battle, but any educated Chinese would know that the music portrays the historical battle between the two great warriors Liu Bang and Xiang Yu in 202 B.C. before Liu

Bang united the nation and established the Han dynasty. The piece depicts the different strategies in the battlefield and the final ambush. The music progresses with the storyline, sometimes depicting calm moments before the battle, sometimes depicting the sound of the wind and crying of the cranes to express the anxiety of the warriors. The *pipa* techniques used to evoke these sounds are fast strumming, glissando, and pitch-bending by pushing and pulling the lefthand fingers. Worked together, these techniques offer a range of sounds to evoke the story of the battle for the listeners. "Shimian maifu" is so famous that, apart from being performed as an unaccompanied solo, it was arranged as a *pipa* concerto to be performed with either a Western symphony orchestra or a Chinese orchestra.

ACTIVITY 2.6   *Listen to CD track 19 and use a graph to chart where you hear sectional change or mood shift, for instance. Then, using the sonic events as a guide, construct a story according to your chart, whether or not your story follows the traditional title. After that, reflect on the usefulness (or not) of a programmatic guide to a piece of music. Write a paragraph stating your conclusion about this.*

Solo Repertory for Guzheng.   At the end of a lecture on Chinese music in a world music class I was teaching and after watching a video clip of a performance, a student approached me to ask whether it was unusual that a Chinese musician used the Japanese *koto* when performing Chinese music. Immediately, I realized that she was confusing the Chinese *guzheng* or *zheng* (Figure 2.9, CD track 20) with the Japanese *koto*. I explained to her that while these two instruments look alike, were used in the imperial court orchestra, and share a common origin and that the Chinese character for the word *koto* is exactly the same word in Japanese, they are not the same. As a result of her confusion, I delved into the early history of the *guzheng* and its relationship to the Japanese *koto*.

The Chinese *guzheng* is a plucked zither with a long history dating back to the Warring States period (475–221 B.C.E.). It was used in court orchestras with other kinds of plucked zithers and was later popularized in the folk and vernacular music outside the court. Around the eighth century, it was adopted in Japan as part of the court and ceremonial music. Over time, the two instruments developed separate identities,

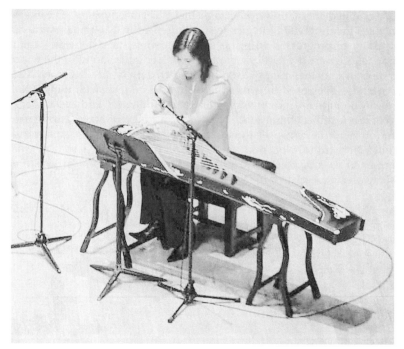

FIGURE 2.9 *Twenty-one stringed plucked zither* guzheng, *CD track 20. The plucked zither is believed to have existed before the Qin dynasty (221–207 B.C.E.). Strings are mounted over triangular-shaped moveable bridges. The right hand plucks the strings while the left hand alters the pitch by pressing and pulling the strings. The present-day standard* guzheng *consists of twenty-one strings, while earlier models have only thirteen or sixteen strings. The* guzheng *is tuned to a pentatonic scale, and the twenty-one stringed model has a range of four octaves. 2003. (Courtesy of Chinese Music Virtuosi)*

construction, and practice. The Japanese *koto* developed into a chamber instrument for solos but mostly as an accompaniment for songs, while the Chinese *guzheng* continued being performed in the court orchestra and as a solo performance instrument. For centuries, the *guzheng* has been figured prominently in painting and in poems, but artists have frequently confused it with the seven-stringed plucked zither, the *guqin* (Figure 2.4), because they are similar in shape.

The traditional *guzheng* has twelve or thirteen strings made of silk. Beginning in the 1950s, steel strings were adopted for durability and volume. Significantly for the music that can be played on it, the number of strings was gradually increased to twenty-one or more after the 1960s. The *guzheng* now has a range of four octaves and is tuned to a pentatonic scale. Tuning can be done by repositioning the moveable bridges for each string. Pitches other than those produced by the open strings can be produced by pressing the string on the lefthand side of the bridge. In playing the *guzheng*, the right fingers pluck the strings while the left hand presses or pulls the string to change the pitches. This subtle pressing of the strings by the left hand has become a unique feature of *guzheng* music. Other playing techniques include plucking inward or outward, tremolos, and glissando.

Similar to the different schools of *pipa* playing style, *guzheng* playing is divided into different regional schools according to playing styles. As stated earlier, regional styles are important in the context of constructing national music because a new solo *guzheng* tradition is formed by incorporating the different playing techniques and repertories as its foundation. There are five different schools of *guzheng* playing, each reflecting the musical characteristics of its respective region. The five schools are Shangtong, Henan, Kejia, Zhejiang, and Chaozhou. Each school is defined by its own performing styles and techniques such as in the use of vibrato, tuning, and the various ways of manipulating sound through the combined use of the left and right hands.

"Yuzhou Wenchang" ("Fishing Boat, Evening Songs," CD track 20), now considered a traditional composition, was composed in 1936 using as a basis a Shandong regional piece called "Shuang ban" ("Double Beat") and its variations. According to a popular interpretation, the music depicts the happy life of a fisherman. The structure of this piece is based on a common practice of thematic development that is used in many regional pieces. The main theme is first stated and followed by a symmetrical phrase that functions as an answer. This musical procedure is called the consequent and antecedent principle of melodic construction. Both phrases share the same melodic motive. This way of constructing melody is viewed by the Chinese scholar Li Minxiong as representative of how *minjian* musicians create new pieces.

ACTIVITY 2.7 *Listen to the CD track 20 and pay particular attention to the opening melody until you have the sound of the instrument in your ears. Then find the sound of a Japanese koto on the Internet and listen to it several times.*

• *Compare the sound of the* guzheng *to that of the Japanese* koto.

• *Focusing on the* guzheng *in CD track 20, count the number of glissandos you can hear and the number of simultaneous pluckings of two strings that occur in this piece.*

In this chapter, I introduced the formation of *guoyue* and outlined how musicians resolved musical and ideological dilemmas that they encountered in the process of creating a new national music. The solution for most was to combine Western music with indigenous practices. However, the sense of a "national music" has changed. After 1949, the resulting music was institutionalized by the state conservatories and performing troupes. New interpretations of old traditions and standardization of performance practice and theories were put in place and disseminated. In addition to these new features, perhaps the most remarkable recent developments are the rapid growth of Chinese orchestra music and instrumental solos. The new trend is to write pieces that require a large orchestra with extra players and to compose virtuoso concerti for a solo instrument and orchestras. Regardless of the instrument, there is a concerto written for it. The number of new solo pieces continues to increase as performers are looking for new compositions to demonstrate their technique. Given these recent changes, the concept of *guoyue* continues to be reshaped and the content will change to keep up with changing visions of Chinese nation and identity.

What "national music" really came to mean is music created since Western music was introduced and the ideological ideas of the communist government caused the creation of new aesthetics—instrumental sound—and practices, including ensemble structure and compositions. Status of musicians changed, institutions were created. What comprises "Chinese music" includes the traditional and more contemporary regional music but also the music for the people—truly a national music.

CHAPTER 3

Regional Musics with the National Soundscape

In response to my question of how he viewed regional music and its place in Chinese music, one of the prominent senior scholars Li Minxiong of the Shanghai Conservatory had this to say:

> Chinese music consists of many regional traditions that are different in form, style, quality, and repertory. While one can say that regional music is the foundation of Chinese music, one needs to make a distinction between *difang yinyue* [regional music] and *minzu* music [national or people's music], or *minyue* for short. *Difang yinyue* is like the raw material from which *minjian yinyue* is developed. It is untreated and unpolished because it is performed by untrained folk or *minjian* musicians. Nowadays there are plenty of *minjian* music activities all over China, but one needs to be careful in order to distinguish the trained and untrained musicians and to scrutinize their musical practice. Although some *minjian* musicians are good players, their playing is casual (*suibian*) and unscientific. They play whatever comes to mind and never bother to write anything down. This is partly because they lack formal training and proper musical knowledge. Because of the association of *difang yinyue* with this kind of musician, *difang yinyue* has in turn been unstructured and unorganized. But with the help of scholars and trained musicians from the conservatories, more *difang yinyue* can be developed and we can have better music. (Extracted from interviews with Li Minxiong by author)

Li's response was revealing and instructive. My musical encounter in the Chaozhou region while looking for local *xianshi* music (see chapter 1) serves as a good example of the tension between regional music and national music. What I discovered there and across the country were two levels of music cultures coexisting and interacting, each with its own purpose, motivation, and practice.

As you are now beginning to realize, China is a large country that contains a large number of diverse regional cultures. Any traveler to China undoubtedly will notice the variety of regional cultures subtly woven into everyday life and affecting rituals, customs, religion, food, clothing, music, and performing arts, among other facets. Regional culture is meaningful and has practical social functions for people within their respective locales but may not be readily intelligible to people outside the immediate area. For most Chinese, their place of origin (that is, their ancestral homeland rather than their place of residence) and regional culture are important identity markers and ways to distinguish themselves from other subethnic groups.

Regional cultures, often tied to specific localities, are sometimes appropriated into national culture for political purposes. The two levels of culture work in opposite ways based on different notions of identity. While regional culture distinguishes one subgroup of people and culture from others, national culture consolidates disparate groups into one entity. Regionalism creates multiple local identities while national culture flattens differences. Given their intrinsic relationship, however, any discussion of national culture without consideration of regional culture will be incomplete and vice versa. In music, the line that distinguishes regional music from national music is elusive because the definition of national music *guoyue* has changed over time (see chapter 2).

Since the national music project stems from the central government and is vigorously promoted and richly supported, Chinese scholars view it as the center or the core of Chinese musical practice, while regional music is considered peripheral and marginal. This hierarchical way of thinking about music obviously affects musicians' attitudes toward regional music. It is a common belief among scholars and composers that regional music in its original form needs to be developed, systematized, and "cleaned up" before it can be utilized or properly appreciated. The notion of development, *fazhan* in Chinese, has been an important motto for musicians since 1949. *Fazhan* in music implies a range of meanings. It includes consistency in tuning and performing styles, music that is composed and written down in notation, predetermined treatment of music, experimentation with new sound, and breaking away from traditions. In short, "to develop" is to transform music according to Western music sensibilities. Based on this notion of development, it is not difficult to understand why musicians in academe disparage regional *minjian* musicians as backward and untrained. My conversation with the senior teacher illustrates a distinct hierarchy in music preference that is internalized and embraced by the conservatory-trained musicians. Understanding regional music or *difang yinyue* from both local and national perspectives is therefore essential to grasping an overall picture of Chinese music. How do the two levels of identity politics manifest themselves in musical terms?

In this chapter, I introduce several prominent regional music genres, focusing particularly on distinctions in three important components: repertory, instrumentation, and performance practice. Language is the fourth component if singing or speech is involved. It is necessary to bear in mind that there is a great deal more interesting regional music out there than I can present in this small volume.

Rather than seeing regional music as distinctly separate from national music, I suggest viewing them as mutually constituted. One cannot exist without the other. For example, the government has played indirect and direct roles in regional music. The government adoption of a more relaxed open door market economy has incidentally fueled the revival of many regional music traditions in their localities in recent years. The development of special economic zones in regions such as Fujian, Shanghai, Guangdong, and Zhejiang has indirectly stimulated interests in local culture among overseas Chinese. For example, many Taiwanese donated money to support *nanguan* or *nanyin* activities in the city of Quanzhou in Fujian province, and Thai-Chinese often return to learn Chaozhou *xianshi* music from local Shantou musicians. The explicit attention of government directed toward regional cultures also increased in recent years. In the 1990s, the Chinese Ministry of Culture worked in conjunction with the national musicians' association and the Music Research Institute to embark on a massive project of collecting all local music by local scholars. The recent publication of volumes of *minjian* music or folk music of all provinces is an excellent example of this kind of national effort to revive regional music. In 2006, fourteen regional music genres were listed as part of a national cultural protection project, bringing further attention to genres that were once considered marginal in the construction of China's national soundscape.

THE CANTON/GUANGDONG REGION

Once considered the "southern barbarians" by Chinese who populated the central plains, the people of Guangdong or Canton were considered uncivilized and inferior to their northern counterparts. The region where they lived, known as Guangdong in the pinyin romanization system or Canton according to the British colonial government, was considered the margins of the Chinese empire. Because this region was considered less than desirable strategically and politically, the government of the Qing dynasty decided to allow foreign traders to conduct business there as a concession of losing the First Opium War (1840–1842) to the British. Ultimately, the cities of Hong Kong and Macau were ceded to Britain and Portugal and became their colonies in the late nineteenth century. While the Chinese negative attitude toward this region lasted until the end of the Qing dynasty (1644–1912), at the turn of the twentieth century its coastal location caused it to become an important port of entry for many foreign merchants. Many foreign businesses had set up their trading posts and liaison offices in this area. A large number of Christian churches also established missions for their evangelical activities. The prevalence of foreign culture there deeply affected Cantonese culture as it tried to respond to the influx of many Western cultural practices.

ACTIVITY 3.1 *If international business particularly interests you, join with a team of friends to plan an oral report on the two concessions that were made by the Chinese government to European nations in the late nineteenth century: Hong Kong (Great Britain) and Macau (Portugal). How was their history similar, and in what ways were they different?*

As a result of massive migration of Cantonese to the Americas and different parts of Asia in the nineteenth century, many people in the West are familiar with Cantonese culture. It is interesting to note that only Chinese have an operative sense of "overseas community" apart from scattered expatriates. Many immigrants continued to establish familial ties in the homeland and even some second or third generations are continued to be recorded in family genealogy and in some extreme cases government census. Many non-Cantonese overseas Chinese communities have adopted Cantonese culture as a part of their own practice. Consequently, Cantonese music has become an important cultural icon in many Chinatowns in the West. What is Cantonese music, and how does it differ from other regional genres?

In China, the term *Guangdong yinyue,* or *Cantonese music,* has two meanings. At one level, it refers to a system of music developed from the areas along the Pearl River Delta. It includes many localized vocal and instrumental traditions. At a more specific level, Guangdong music refers to a type of instrumental ensemble music developed there since the 1920s. The following section focuses on three representative genres from the system of Guangdong music—Guangdong *yinyue* (instrumental music), Guangdong opera or *yueju,* and the narrative song genre *nanyin* that occurs in operas—in order to show the diversity of music from this region.

Instrumental Music: Guangdong **Yinyue.**   A type of localized *sizhu* (silk and bamboo) music developed in the Guangdong regions that absorbed influences from northern theatrical and instrumental musics. It has been popular as entertainment music since the eighteenth century. Before the 1920s, the most common ensemble was known as *wujiatou* (literally, "five frames") or the "hard bow" ensemble. This five-piece ensemble consisted of a combination of bowed and plucked lutes and a wind instrument. The strings included the high-pitched two-stringed lute *erxian* (Figure 1.14, CD track 13), a *tiqin* (similar to a *banhu*), a *sanxian* (Figure 1.6, CD track 5), and a *yueqin* (Figure 1.7, CD track 6). The wind instrument was a *dizi* (Figure 1.9, CD track 8), but was called *hengxiao* (horizontal *xiao,* not to be confused with the vertical flute *xiao*) in Cantonese. After the 1920s, this instrumental combination was reduced to only three instruments—*gaohu, qinqin* and *yangqin*—as musicians were seeking to produce a mellower sound because of changing musical taste and sonic ideals (see chapter 1). The high-pitched bowed lute *erxian* was replaced by the Cantonese *gaohu.* Because of the soft and lyrical timbre of these instruments, the new three-piece ensemble is called the "soft bow" ensemble. This ensemble eventually formed the basis of all Cantonese music ensembles, but extra instruments such as the vertical *xiao,* the *yehu* (coconut-shelled bowed lute), and the *pipa* were sometimes added according to the performance context and desired quality of the music.

Because of Canton's unique cultural milieu and its proximity to the then-British colony of Hong Kong, Cantonese music was able to develop in the flourishing recording and movie industry, night clubs, and live entertainment venues. New trends were set especially by players/composers in order to satisfy an increasing domestic and overseas demand for more new music. Western instruments such the violin, Hawaiian slide guitar, banjo, xylophone, and saxophone began to be used in Cantonese music since the 1920s. The *gaohu* and *yangqin* gradually assumed a prominent position in the ensemble. Other strings instruments such as the *zhongruan* and *zhonghu* were also added to fill in the middle register of the ensemble. This is an excellent example of how a regional Chinese music modernized under the influence of its environment and its location. Figure 3.1 is a cover of a Cantonese music publication circulated in Guangzhou and Hong Kong in the 1940s. It is obvious from the picture that the practice of using microphones, violins, trombones, and both cipher and Western notation in Cantonese music was no stranger to the general public for which the publication was targeted.

Innovations in Guangdong music have been attributed to several prominent musicians since the 1930s, among them Lu Wencheng (1895–1961), Qiu Hechou (1880–1942), Yan Laolie (1832–?), and He Liutang

FIGURE 3.1   *A cover of a 1940s Cantonese music publication showing the use of Western instruments and notation. (Courtesy of Frederick Lau)*

(1870–1934). These musicians were active in Canton, Hong Kong, Macau, and other cities whose populations were primarily Cantonese, and some of their best-known pieces have become classic in the Cantonese repertory. A few such as Lu and Qiu also authored collections of Guangdong music and instrumental method books. Qiu has been regarded as the promoter of the Guangdong style of *yangqin* playing (see Figure 1.8, CD track 7).

The characteristics of Cantonese music are its upbeat tempo, unique melodic leaps, elaborate melodic ornaments in the beginning and ending of the phrases, and use of a scale with the fourth degree of a scale raised a quarter-note and the seventh degree lowered a quarter-tone, creating a sense of "out-of-tuneness" for the uninitiated listeners. Since the 1950s, *gaohu*'s piercing and nasal timbre has become the sonic signature of Cantonese music. CD track 21 is a popular Cantonese instrumental piece, "Double Lament" ("Shuang sheng han"). CD track 22, "The Geese Landing on the Flat Sand" ("Luoyan pingsha"), is an important Cantonese piece with a *suona* (CD track 11) as the leading instrument.

ACTIVITY 3.2   *Listen to CD track 21 and follow along with the leading* gaohu *part. As a performance convention, musicians usually would embellish the melodic line on the spur of the moment during performance. Try to listen to the music and notice the changes that were made to the original melodic line on notes with an asterisk marked above them.*

"Double Lament" ("Shuang sheng han") (CD track 21)

0 54 2 5 4 2̇4̇ | 1 2̇1̇ 7̇ 1 2̇ 5 7571 | 2 5 454̇2̇ 1 2̇ 121̇7̇|5 5 5 5 1 2 4̇5̇ 2|

0 0 65 4·5 2·5 | 4 2̇ 4245 2 4 242̇1̇ | 7 7 21̇ 7 7 7 71 |2 4 242̇5̇ 7124 1 6|

7·124 1 5 7·124 12 7̇ | 6 6765 4 5 212̇4̇ | 5 2124 5·4 5| etc.

After you finish this activity, follow the same procedure and mark the melodic changes that appear on the notation of the piece "The Geese Landing on the Flat Sand" ("Luoyan pingsha") (CD track 22) given below.

Music Notation

Luoyan pingsha

雁 落 平 沙

1 = C 4/4   ♩ = 64   古曲

5 1 6561 5 │ 4·6 5 1761 2 │ 2 4·6 5 1761 ‖: 2 5 4 *3432 1·235 │

2·3 2 3 2327 │ 6 176 5·2 76 │ 1·3 23 5 6 1 2 │ 2 1 2 4·6 │

5 ii 6165 456i │ 5·6i 5 6 5 │ 4 4 5 6 5 176i │ 5·6i 56 5 │

1 — 5 432 │ 1· 2 1 2 1276 │ 5 2 76 1 │ i 1 2 4·6 │

┌─1.──────────────────────────────── ┌─2.──────

5 i i 65 456i │ 5 4 5 1761 2 │ 2 4·6 5 1761 :‖ 5 i i 6 5 456i │ 5 — — 0‖

*Music starts here

Finally, describe in your own words the different emotional impact of the two pieces. How are they different in terms of dynamics, density, and overall mood? How is the timbre of the suona different from that of the bowed lute gaohu?

Opera: **Yueju.**   If you have ever toured the Chinatown of San Francisco or New York, it is likely you heard the sound of Cantonese opera spilling out from upstairs units of older commercial buildings. Cantonese opera or *yueju* is a musical theatrical form popularized in the Guangdong and Guangxi provinces (Figure 1.2, west of the Guangdong province) whose documented history is about two centuries old. Like other Guangdong music genres, the origin of the southern Cantonese opera owes much to northern genres. Chinese music scholars speculate that many traveling theatrical troupes came to perform in the area because Guangdong was a center of trade and commerce. These troupes eventually settled in the region and gradually transformed their music by incorporating regional music in order to cater to local tastes. During the mid-nineteenth century Cantonese opera practitioners replaced northern dialects with local Cantonese dialect and used ordinary vocal quality in combination with the common heightened, falsetto vocal style compared to most northern operas (CD track 23; compare to CD track 17).

Influenced by northern operatic traditions, the percussion sections of the orchestra are similar to those in *jingju, kunqu* opera from East Central

China, and other regional operatic traditions. The conductor of the orchestra is the player of the *bangu* drum, the liaison between the actions on stage and the ensemble. While observing the action on stage, he sets the tempo and signals the other musicians to enter or to finish. His role is similar to that of a Western conductor except that he conducts throughout the entire opera by way of various rhythmic patterns on the *bangu* rather than arm motions. Cueing is therefore aural rather than visual.

The percussion section consists of a flat drum *bangu*, a woodblock, a small gong (*xiao luo*), a big gong (*da luo*), small cymbals (*xiao bo*), a big cymbal (*da bo*), and bells of various sizes (Figure 1.13). The percussionists perform multiple functions for the production. They indicate entrances and exits, punctuate sentences, emphasize words and emotional situations, perform as an interlude between scenes and actions, accompany action and fight scenes, and signal the start or ending of the melodic instruments. Given these important functions, percussion is considered central in the orchestra. This is a unique feature of all Chinese opera production.

The other section of the orchestra is the melodic ensemble. Characteristic of most regional opera, there is one leading melodic instrument that functions as the primary accompaniment to the main vocal line and its player is the group leader of the melodic section. For example, in *jingju* the main melodic accompaniment is the high-pitched *jinghu* (Figure 1.4). In *kunqu* opera it is the side-blown flute *dizi*. In Cantonese opera, the main melodic accompanying instrument is the *gaohu* or *erhu*, in some instances substituted by a violin or saxophone. The rest of the Cantonese opera orchestra, as in Guangdong instrumental music, consists of *yangqin, yueqin, zhonghu, zhongruan, sanxian, pipa, dizi,* and *suona*. Since the 1930s, Western instruments such as the violin, saxophone, or banjo have been utilized (Figure 3.2).

There are three types of vocal production in Cantonese opera, and each one is associated with the gender of the role. The first, *ping hou* ("ordinary voice"), refers to singing with ordinary voice without falsetto. Usually most young male roles and the role of an older woman are sung in *ping hou*, whether they are sung by an actor or actress. CD track 23 is a recording of the 1950s actress Xu Liuxian (Figure 3.3), who was celebrated for her *ping hou* singing. The second is *zi hou* ("boy's voice"); all female roles sing *zi hou* (CD track 24). Third, *da hou* ("big voice") is the voice type for strong male and martial characters (CD track 25).

In terms of music, there are three types of song in Cantonese opera: *banghuang* aria music, narrative songs, and *qupai* fixed titled tunes. All have varying degrees of melodic and textual content.

FIGURE 3.2   *Cantonese orchestral ensemble.* *(Courtesy of Yu Siuwah)*

FIGURE 3.3   *Famous Cantonese actress Xu Liuxian, known for singing* ping hou. *(Courtesy of Yu Siuwah)*

Banghuang. According to Chinese music scholar Bell Yung (1989) there are about thirty different *banghuang* aria types. Each aria type has its own music and textual structure but the song based on the aria type is not titled but by the length of the lines and the accompaniment patterns.

Narrative Songs. Narrative songs are mostly oriented toward the spoken word with relatively little melodic content. They are usually "sung" in a speaking manner and are accompanied by simple beats in the background (CD track 23). In this example, there are several local genres of vocal music each governed by special textual patterns and accompaniment styles.

Qupai. These are songs based on existing melodies that have been widely played across China. Each has a title, specific melody, and meter. When writing a new piece using an existing *qupai,* the composer will have to work carefully to fit the appropriate lyrics into the melody. This presents an interesting dilemma for composers because Chinese language is a tonal language. In tonal language, the meaning of a word changes according to different inflexion. The art of composing lies in the skill of filling in the slot with the appropriate words to fit its melodic and linguistic context (CD track 24).

ACTIVITY 3.3 *CD track 23 is an example of a Cantonese opera song based on the* qupai *"Double Lament" ("Shuang sheng han"), as heard on CD track 21. In this activity, the task is to compare the treatment of the melody between the two versions. First refresh your memory by listening to CD track 21 and then listen to the music again with the notation given in Activity 3.2. After you have done that, listen to CD track 24. Try to listen first without the notation and then follow it with the notation given in Activity 3.2. Finally, take notes on the following points: (1) the difference between the instrumental and vocal melody, (2) the timbre between the vocal and the instrumental part, and (3) the tempo and accompaniment of each rendition.*

BEIJING OPERA: *JINGJU*

Beijing opera, *jingju,* is a regional opera popularized in the capital of China (Figure 1.2). It is perhaps the most celebrated Chinese music inside and outside China (CD track 26). Discussing Chinese opera without mentioning *jingju* would be almost like discussing Anglophone popular music without mentioning the Beatles or Elvis Presley. The twentieth century *jingju* actor Mei Langfang (1894–1961), a male actor who was famous for performing female roles, first brought *jingju* to the world outside China and was thought to have influenced the European playwright Bertolt Brecht (1898–1956). *Jingju* has also been the subject of many recent academic studies as well as theatrical productions that include the play *M Butterfly* by David Henry Hwang (1989) and the motion picture *Farewell My Concubine* by Chinese director Chen Kaige (1993). The University of Hawai'i at Mānoa Asian Theater Program has been producing Beijing opera once every three years on a regular basis since the 1980s. Many amateur *jingju* clubs are thriving throughout China and in many overseas Chinese communities. Clearly, *jingju* continues to fascinate audiences and scholars both inside and outside China.

This genre was popularized during the Qing dynasty (1644–1912), and it became a favorite entertainment of the imperial household. Under the reign of the Empress Dowager (1835–1908), *jingju* was developed further because of the royal patronage. To provide music and opera for the royalty, a theater was built inside the Forbidden City. Besides training musicians and performers in the court, the imperial court also summoned regional troupes to perform in their styles at the palace. In turn, these experiences of regional musicians helped to promote the popularity of *jingju* across the country.

How is the music of *jingju* different from that of Cantonese opera? The distinct regional identity of *jingju* comes from two musical elements—language and music—but both of them demonstrate interplay of regional and national culture. *Jingju* is performed in the local Beijing (Peking) dialect that is now known as Mandarin. Initially, Mandarin was spoken primarily by speakers of the region, but it was eventually adopted as the national language. Likewise *jingju* was adopted as the national opera. These transformations are related to the position of Beijing as the capital and the nation's cultural center.

Other than language, the sonic marker of *jingju is* the use of the high-pitched bowed lute *jinghu* as the main accompaniment. The unique sound of this instrument gives *jingju* its special quality that is easily identifiable from other regional opera. The melodic section in the *jingju* ensemble is led by the *jinghu* and it supported by a few other plucked strings like the *yueqin, pipa, sanxian,* and *zhongruan.* They provide melodic accompaniments to the singing. Although the role and function of the orchestra are similar to those of Cantonese opera, the tone quality, performance technique, terminology, melodic material, organization, and much of the instrumentation are different.

> **ACTIVITY 3.4** *Listen to CD tracks 23 and 26 one after the other. Using the notes from Activity 3.3 as your guide, chart the flow of CD track 26 in terms of changing texture, speed, and vocal accompaniment. Compare and contrast the sound of* jingju *(CD track 26) with Cantonese opera (CD track 23). Pay close attention to the instrumental accompaniment to the singing, the percussion section, and the quality of the voice. Take note of anything strikingly different about them. Then write up your analytical observations about them.*

As you can hear in CD track 26, the *jingju* orchestra is also divided into melodic and percussion sections. And likewise, the *bangu* player in the percussion section is the conductor of the group. As a common practice for learning percussion patterns practiced across China, the *jingju* percussion patterns are represented by a strings of syllables such as *ba* (B), *da* (D), *te* (T), *kuang, ce,* and *cete,* where each sound refers to a single percussion instrument or a combination of instruments. Each rhythmic pattern is identified by a name that implies a combination of phonetic sounds indicating the rhythm and instrumentation. For instance, *kuang* (K) refers to a beat played by all instruments, *te* (t) is the beat played only by the small gong, and so on, as noted below. The rhythmic pattern called *jijifeng* ("A Gust of Wind") contains the following syllables (CD track 27):

‖ B | B̲D̲ T̲ ‖ K | C ‖ K̲ | C̲‖ K̲ | K | C | K‖

repeat as long as needed
from slow to fast

The rhythm is:

Single letter with no line = one count
One line underneath two letters = two sounds played as half-counts
Two lines underneath two letters = two sounds played as quarter-counts
Vertical lines separate groups of beats (here, groups of two beats)

The syllables representing percussion strokes are:

B = *ba,* right hand on the flat drum
D = *da,* left hand on the flat drum
K = *kuang,* played by small cymbal, small gong, big gong, and flat drum
T = *te,* played by small gong *xiao luo* only
C = *ce,* small cymbal *bo* only
0 = rest, usually no sound

ACTIVITY 3.5 *You can build your own* jingju *percussion section with friends. Find equivalent instruments for the flat drum, small gong, small cymbal, and large gong. Pay close attention to saying the syllables for* jijifeng *(CD track 27) as a group repeatedly.*

‖ B | BD T ‖ K | C ‖ K | C ‖ K | K | C | K ‖
|----------|

repeat as long as needed
from slow to fast

Then divide the parts among you and add in one instrument at a time to the group. Continue the process until everybody is playing and saying the syllables at the same time. Since the tempo of the percussion pattern depends on the action on stage, the pattern can be slow or fast. You can practice slowing down and speeding up the pattern. When you have perfected this pattern, try another pattern called "Fengdiantou" ("Phoenix Nodding Its Head"). Again learn to say the pattern fluently before attempting to play. Add one instrument at a time. After you can play the entire pattern, you can play the two patterns one after the other. The pattern is represented as follows:

‖ 0 BD T | K· D C T| K TC KT|K 0|

Vocal music is set in one of two commonly used aria types, *xipi* and *erhuang.* Each aria type contains specific beat patterns or meters and melodic features that include cadential tone, melodic turns, mode, and tonal center. These aria types are unique and different from those found in Cantonese opera in terms of concepts and performance practice. The mood of *xipi* is lively and cheerful (CD track 26), whereas *erhuang* (CD track 28) is spirited and heroic and with a different tuning on the *jinghu* (CD track 29). Both types of arias can be sung in a variety of tempos, which are indicated by the term *ban,* literally meaning "clappers," but the term is also used to refer to the metrical arrangement and tempo. This variety of *ban* ranges from fast to slow, each of which can accommodate syllabic passages where every word is sung to a specific note and melismatic rubato sections where one word can be sung to many notes.

Training to be a *jingju* performer takes years of intense training. This includes acting, physical training, makeup, dialogue, movements, and gesture, all of which are related to each of the role types. The characters, which indicate age and social status, are young female (*dan*), young male (*sheng*), painted face (*jing*), and clown or comic character (*chou*). In addition to the facial makeup and costumes, each stock character is characterized by one vocal style and is identified by timbre, voice quality, volume, and manner of enunciation. Performers often specialized in a single role during their careers.

The most expressive of the voices is usually concentrated on the two principal roles *sheng* and *dan*. Performers of the *dan* role usually sing in a stylized falsetto fashion, regardless of whether the role is played by a woman or a man. *Dan* is often the character of a young woman who is virtuous, filial, emotional, skilled in fighting, and romantic. The actor Mei Langfang is famous for his performance of *dan* roles. *Sheng* describes a man who is young, cultivated, refined, and scholarly. The voice quality is equivalent to that of a tenor but is more nasal. *Jing,* whose character is represented by colorful makeup covering the whole face, portrays a man of power, courage, righteousness, and action. His vocal quality is strong and thunderous. *Chou,* played as a villain, corrupt official, or petty criminal, is a comic character whose role is entertaining in nature. His singing style is shrill and close to colloquial speech patterns.

Regional operas are usually popular among people from the region. The actors and musicians of each genre generally do not cross over to perform in another tradition, and fans of one genre rarely delve into other regional genres. However, this generalization does not apply to *jingju*. Since it emerged as a national opera in the early twentieth century, *jingju* has been performed and taught all over the country. With the support of the government, *jingju* troupes continue to thrive across the country and in Taiwan (Guy 2005).

What is interesting, however, is that in recent years the Chinese Academy is presenting Chinese opera as having many regional variations.

Students there are required to learn about different regional styles, which has resulted in the blurring of the once rigid lines that distinguish one genre from the other.

FUJIAN: NARRATIVE *NANGUAN* VOCAL AND INSTRUMENTAL GENRE

A few-hour bus ride from Guangdong province heading northeast takes you to the neighboring Fujian province, where the language and culture are different. Fujian, also known previously as Fukien or Hokkien, is a short distant across the Taiwan Strait from Taiwan (Figure 1.2). This area is historically significant for its role in China's maritime trade. The famous Ming dynasty (1368–1644) maritime navigator Zheng He stopped twice in Fujian province during his influential voyages to Southeast Asia and to the Middle East. Memories of him live on in Fujian, and you can still find shrines honoring him in the area. Evidence of the area's contact with foreign culture includes one of the earliest mosques in China founded in the city of Quanzhou. Like Guangdong province, Fujian was an important trading center that was opened to Western nations after the First Opium War in mid-nineteenth century. Among Fujian's most famous cities are Xiamen (formerly known as Amoy), Quanzhou, and Fuzhou (presently the provincial capital).

Fujian province is best known for a number of musical genres that are believed by scholars to have histories dating back to the Tang (618–907 C.E.) and Song (960–1279 C.E.) dynasties. They include *nanguan, liyuan* opera, *gaojia* opera, and *putian* opera. Many of these genres are still performed today. In this section, I focus on the narrative *nanguan,* a genre for which Fujian people are famous (Figure 3.5, CD track 30). At the time of this writing, *nanguan* had just been designated by the PRC government as one of the twenty-four officially protected genres of "Intangible Cultural Heritage." This will be interesting because it demonstrates further the regional and national nexus of Chinese music. The attention to *nanguan* has promoted its reputation, and *nanguan* is frequently presented at national and international conferences (Figure 3.4). As a regional genre, *nanguan* has been elevated to become an art form that can be performed in concerts and as a national cultural treasure.

Nanguan—literally, "southern pipe"—is a unique vocal music with instrumental accompaniment. Also called *nanyin* ("southern sound"), *nanguan*'s origin can be linked to elite court music and the lyric poetry *ci* of the Song period (960–1278 C.E.). The surviving collections of *nanguan* music confirm that *nanguan* has existed since the middle of the Ming

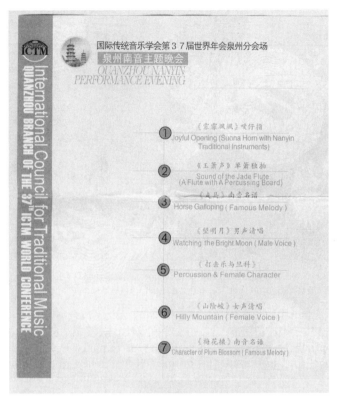

FIGURE 3.4 *A program of* nanguan *music presented as part of the 37th World Conference of the International Council for Traditional Music in Quanzhou, Fujian Province. 2004.* (Courtesy of Frederick Lau)

dynasty in the sixteenth century. Because of *nanguan*'s classical roots and history, it has been accepted by local scholars and musicians as a musical tradition of the literati class of the region. *Nanguan* is performed in many public places such as parks and teahouses and in privates venues such as music clubs or community centers. The present-day *nanguan* was developed in the southern city of Quanzhou, a place with a long history of interacting with foreign culture, including a visit by Marco Polo.

Nanguan is derived from the textual musical form *ci*, roughly translated as a sung ballad. *Ci* was written in vernacular language, different from the rigid formal structure and rhyme scheme of classical Chinese

FIGURE 3.5 *Amateur* nanguan *performance in Quanzhou. Notice the placement of the performers and instruments. From left:* sanxian, pipa, *singer with* paiban, dongxiao, *and* tiqin. *1987.* (Courtesy of Frederick Lau)

poetry. Because of this, *ci* were somewhat free and expressive and appropriate for narrating ancient tales of romance in which human emotions and love were the primary focus. When put in a musical setting, *ci* evoked extreme emotions with poetic imagery and lament. This particular relationship between music and text is where *nanguan*'s beauty and creativity lie.

There are three subcategories of music within the *nanguan* repertory. *Zhi* constitutes large vocal and instrumental suites made up of several individual pieces or sections. Each suite contains lyrics, music scores for the vocal, and *pipa* tablature. *Pu* is programmatic instrumental pieces that are grouped in suites. The number of pieces in each suite range from three to ten. *Qu* are short vocal and instrumental pieces, each set in a specific meter with melodic characteristics and mode. There is a consistent quality to the entire repertory, however, because all the pieces are set primarily in a pentatonic (five-pitch) scale with occasional added notes and the meter is basically duple or multiple. In order to accommodate the rhythm of the text, a predetermined concept of melodic mode called *guanmen* is used. Each *guanmen* provides important melodic content for the piece and is also used a classification device for the repertory.

According to historical collections of *nanguan* music that still survive, this genre of music has been notated and anthologized since the sixteenth century. These collections provide a treasure trove of textual and musical information for present-day practitioners and scholars. The text usually appears in larger print with musical information written in smaller font below the text. The music is written in a type of *gongche* notation (Figure 2.6) that provides metric markings, *pipa* melody, and *pipa* finger techniques in different columns. Similar to the Chinese writing system, the columns are read from right to left and starting from the top down.

A *nanguan* ensemble usually consists of four to five instrumentalists and a singer (Figure 3.5, CD track 30). The principle instrument of the ensemble is the pear-shaped plucked lute *pipa* (Figure 1.5). The *nanguan pipa* is similar to the style of the Tang dynasty *pipa* or the Japanese *biwa* in *gagaku* music, which also has a bent beck and is held horizontally. These features that existed only in older versions of the *pipa* are evidence of the long history of *nanguan*.

ACTIVITY 3.6   *The* pipa *is an instrument that was imported from Central Asia to China and Japan during the Tang dynasty. Although the modern* pipa *is different from the earlier models, the* pipa *used in* nanguan *and Japan continue to be modeled on earlier construction, which features a bent neck. Go to the Internet and find as many photos and drawings of Japanese* biwa, Tang pipa, *and* nanguan pipa *as possible. Give a short report on the similarities and differences between the three types of* pipa.

The only wind instrument of the ensemble is a vertical flute *xiao*, which is called *dongxiao* by local musicians. The *dongxiao* has a larger bore than the regular *xiao* and is the predecessor of the Japanese *shakuhachi* (Wade 2005: pp. 49–55). The *dongxiao* elaborates on the melody and plays more notes than the other instruments. This instrument is accompanied by a two-stringed bowed lute *erxian*. In addition to the *pipa*, there are other types of stringed instruments such *erxian* and *sanxian* (Figure 1.6, CD track 5), the long-necked plucked lute. These instruments play the melody in a different lower octave than the *pipa*. Each instrument performs a version of the main vocal line but also embellishes it with ornaments idiomatic to the instrument, producing a heterophonic texture similar to that of *jiangnan sizhu* and *xianshi* (chapter 1). Sometimes a small double-reed *suona* (Figure 1.12), known to indigenous musicians as *yü'ai,* is also added. The singer directs this ensemble by beating time with the *paiban,* a percussion instrument consisting of several pieces of hard wooden pieces attached together at the top.

All *nanguan* pieces are sung in the Fujian dialect of Quanzhou city by one singer, regardless of the storyline and the number of characters in the story. To enhance the refined quality of the music, each note has to be articulated clearly in the beginning of each word, as you can notice in CD track 30. Because the tempo of the music is relatively slow, singers need to manipulate their pronunciation to prolong the vowels after the initial consonant. These vocal effects are produced by opening and closing the oral cavity and by involving the nasal, guttural, and dental areas for tone production. The attention to the refined quality is matched by the tightly controlled tone quality produced on the *pipa* and other bowed strings. Unlike singing in many other cultures, vibrato is not used and each sound has to be pure, steady, full, and round. It is often sung with the mouth half-closed, and some sounds have to be made with a completely closed mouth.

ACTIVITY 3.7 Nanguan *music is based on four-beat rhyth-mic cycle, but that can be extended to sixteen beats, depending on the form. The beginning of the cycle is marked by a beat on the* paiban. *When listening to the music, it is useful to follow the* paiban *beat and count from 1 to 4 at the beginning of each measure. Listen to CD track 30 and follow along with the first* paiban *beat starting at 0:23, which is preceded by a free introduc-tion played by the* dongxiao. *Since the singer usually needs to manipulate the sound and stretch the syllables, each beat may need to be subdivided into four smaller beats. Try either 1—2—3—4, or put more space in between each main beat, such as 1-(ee-and-a)-2-(ee-and-a)-3-(ee-and-a)-4-(ee-and-a). The tempo of the music is somewhat flexible. In other words, some beats may be later than expected. Listen all the way through CD track 30, keeping the beat.*

Here I give the timing for the opening articulation of each word of the text in CD track 30. Although the words are sung in Quanzhou dialect, I use the pinyin transliteration to approximate the lyric. This is because Quanzhou dialect is very different from Mandarin and other regional dialects, and some of the sounds unique to that region cannot be reproduced accurately. Listen again to CD track 30, paying special attention to how the vowel of each word is being manipulated and elongated by the changing shape of the mouth. The dotted line following each initial sound indicates a melismatic melodic line on a sustained vowel. A rough translation of the text reads as follows: "The winter sky is cold and the mountain fills with snow. I am sitting inside by myself, feeling cold and lonely."

0:00–0:10	Single note on the pipa, starts slow and gradually getting faster	
0:10–0:12	Dongxiao enters	
0:12–0:19	Vocal starts with "Da—an"	[winter]
0:20	"Uuh"	
0:27–35	"Tian——"	[sky]
0:36–46	"Gu———a"	[cold]
0:47–0:53	"Xi———"	[snow]
0:54–0:57	"Moi——an"	[filled]
0:58–1:02	"Uuh——"	
1:03–1:08	"Shua——"	[mountain]
1:09–1:15	"Chua—lrung"	[humble people]
1:16–1:24	"Yi–am–huei"	[close door]
1:25–1:26	"Zi"	[only]
1:27–1:32	"Da—do—"	[alone]
1:33–1:39	"Zi———"	[myself]
1:40–1:46	"Ging———"	[more]
1:47–1:56	"Gua———"	[cold]

THE *JIANGNAN* AREA ENSEMBLE
MUSIC: *JIANGNAN SIZHU*

As described in chapter 1, *jiangnan sizhu*, literally, "silk and bamboo music" from south of the Yangtze River, refers to the string and wind ensemble music popularized in East Central China, around the Jiangsu and Zhejiang provinces (CD track 1). As a regional music genre, *jiangnan*

sizhu was initially popularized among the urban literati and later became a favorite genre for local amateur musicians. *Jiangnan sizhu* is performed mostly in public venues like teahouses for the enjoyment of musicians. Because of the large number of studies on this genre by scholars inside and outside China, *jiangnan sizhu* has become perhaps the best-known regional music of China. In recent years, this music is also beginning to be performed by professional musicians and in the conservatories. Because of its popularity, the city of Shanghai has sponsored several important international *jiangnan sizhu* events (Figure 3.6).

By now, you are thoroughly familiar with the instruments used in *jiangnan sizhu* as introduced in chapter 1. The repertory is commonly said to consist of eight famous pieces, known collectively as "badaqu" ("Eight Big Pieces"). The names of the eight pieces are (1) "Zhonghua liuban" ("Moderate Tempo Six Beats"), (2) "Sanliu" ("Three Six"), (3) "Xingjie" ("Street Procession"), (4) "Huan le ge" ("Song of Happiness"), (5) "Sihe ruyi" ("Four Together, as You Wish"), (6) "Yunqing" ("Cloud Celebration"), (7) "Manliu ban" ("Slow Six Beats"), and (8) "Man sanliu" ("Slow Three Six"). While these eight pieces are the

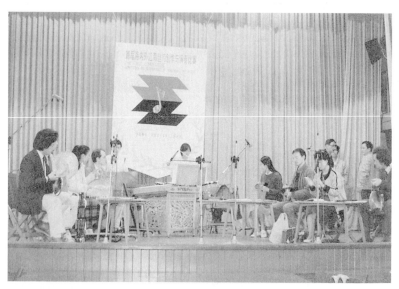

FIGURE 3.6 *This photo features a group of foreign students from the Shanghai Conservatory performing at a concert during the First International Competition of* jiangnan sizhu *held in Shanghai. 1987. (Courtesy of Frederick Lau)*

core pieces of the genre, there are many other smaller or subsidiary pieces in the repertory.

During my stay in Shanghai, I visited teahouses almost every day to learn this music. When I asked Mr. Zhou Wei, a member of a prominent family of *jiangnan sizhu* performers, whether musicians would get tired of playing pieces from the same repertory over and over again, he smiled and told me that as long as a player knows the rules for playing this music, one would find this music exciting instead of boring. So what are the rules?

Playing *jiangnan sizhu* relies on collective efforts; no individual part should stand out like a solo. Each player performs his version of the melody by altering it, being expected to compose or "improvise" on the spot. Although altering the main melody is highly individualized, the parts have to be performed in relationship to the others. Zhou's rule of thumb is always to yield to other players in the spirit of collaboration. When someone is performing a complicated version of the melody, others should stay clear and not be in direct conflict. When someone is shifting to a higher register, others should go the opposite direction in order to create a sense of balance. According to Zhou, it is only when players observe these simple rules that they can maintain the excitement and liveliness of the music.

An important concept of elaboration often cited by musicians is *fangman jiahua,* literally, "making slow and adding flowers." *Fangman jiahua* refers to expanding the melody by adding more notes or compressing the melody by reducing notes. When applied to the repertory, this process creates different versions of a piece that sound appreciably different from the original and are called by a new name. Individual performers can also make use of this process as a general principle guiding their playing. When the tempo is going fast, a player can drop notes so that he can play faster and also clarify the texture. When the tempo is slow, there is more time to add notes to the existing melody. This process is sometimes known as recomposition, a practice that is attributed to *minjian* musicians.

ACTIVITY 3.8 *This notation shows how a new version called "Zhonghua liuban" is related to the original tune called "Liuban." The new version is played twice as fast so that more notes can be accommodated within any given time. Listen to CD track 31 and follow the notation given here. First pay close attention to the upper and lower line separately and then focus on how the two parts are related.*

```
"Liuban"    ‖3                3    | 6                2                          |
"Zhonghua"  ‖3      --    | 3. 2 5. 3 | 6      --      |2  5   32 |

‖1          --    | 5          5    |

‖1  1  0 35 | 2327 6. 123 | 5. 6 3 2 |5 3      0 23 |

‖1                | 6          1    |

‖1217  662 | 1761  221 | 3235  6213 | 5.617  6235 |
```

REGIONAL VARIANTS OF A WIDESPREAD ENSEMBLE MUSIC: *LUOGU* AND *CHUIDA*

Luogu and *chuida,* usually played together, is the collective name for any percussion and wind ensemble, a popular instrumental combination found throughout China. It is called by the names *chuida* ("blow and struck"), *guchui* ("drum and blow"), and occasionally simply *luogu* ("gongs and drum"). Each regional style is identified by the name of the region from which it came, with the name of the region first, as in *Zhejiang chuida* (Figure 3.7), *Sunan chuida, Liaonan guchui,* and so on. These ensembles are different from the regional music examples discussed earlier, which are performed indoors with a soft and refined quality of sound. Because of their contemplative and subdued tone quality, such ensembles usually are not suitable for performing outdoors or in street processions.

Chinese director Chen Kaige opens his 1985 movie *Yellow Earth* with a scene in which a wind and percussion ensemble is seen at a wedding procession while the bride is being carried in a sedan chair across the hill to the groom's house. In the first few minutes, the *suona* leads the ensemble playing a continuous melody accented by the drum, cymbals, and gongs. The music and ensemble are typical of northwestern China. The function of the ensemble is to enhance the festive atmosphere for the occasion by making lots of sound.

Like all regional ensembles, the instrumentation and performance styles vary from region to region, defined by unique musical characteristics. All ensembles consist of two components: melodic and rhythmic. The melodic part is usually played either by a single wind

FIGURE 3.7 *Picture of a local Zhejiang wind and drum ensemble. Front row from left: a pair of drums, two* suona *players also on* sanxian; *back row:* erhu. *1987. (Courtesy of Frederick Lau)*

instrument or a combination of winds such as *suona, sheng, guangzi,* or *dizi.* The percussion instruments, similar to those found in regional operas, include gongs, cymbals *bo,* and drums. The rhythmic cycle is played on a group of percussion instruments such as a variety of gongs, cymbals, drums, and woodblocks.

In *chuida* music, the organizing principle is centered on the interaction between the melodic and rhythmic parts. In some regions such as the southern Jiangsu province and Chaozhou region, both the percussion and the melody part can be played as solo sections within a piece. However, the most exciting aspect of *chuida* and *luogu chuida* music is found in the way the two parts alternate. Each regional style is defined by a specific rhythmic pattern and melodic cycle. For example, in Hebei province, the wind ensemble uses the double-reed *guangzi* as the principal instrument, the melodic part is made up of a series of variations of the main melody, and the percussion provides basic accompaniment. But in *Sunan chuida,* Shanxi province's "Eight Big Suites" ("badatao"), and *Chaozhou luogu,* the percussion and melodic parts are equal, and players of both perform solo sections.

ACTIVITY 3.9 *If you listen carefully to CD track 32, you will notice how the two groups trade off within a piece. This piece, based on a fixed tune labeled "Qupai," is called "Chuang jiangling" and is from Jiangnan area. The main melody consists of a four-bar phrase (or a total of sixteen beats), and the piece is founded on this melodic motive. The wind group in this example is made up of different sizes of* dizi, sheng, *and* suona. *The percussion is made up of different sizes of cymbals, gongs, and drums. At 1:46, the original melody returns and is similar to the beginning, but the accompaniment is different. At 2:36, the repetition is more literal. Repetition is a standard procedure in wind and drum music because the length of a piece as performed depends on the duration of the social function.*

Follow this sequence of musical events in "Chuang jiangling" (CD track 32):

0:00–030	*Slow introduction, melody played by a group of winds and accompanied by the drums and percussion— eight measures (thirty-two beats)*
0:31–0:40	*Five measures of drum and percussion*
0:31–1:00	*Main theme consisting of ten measures*
1:01–1:15	*Repetition of the melody with* sheng, dizi *with cymbal and drum*
1:16–1:30	*Big drum and* suona *join in*
1:31–1:39	*Melodic and rhythmic parts trade off, creating a dialogue*
1:40–1:45	Sheng *and* dizi *double the notes*
1:46–2:10	*Melodic and rhythmic part trade off*
2:11–2:35	*Percussion solo with woodblock providing a regular beat*
2:36–3:30	*The original melody returns as in the beginning*
3:31–3:51	*Tempo speeds up; the small cymbal provides a regular beat*
3:52–4:00	*Sudden slowing down of the concluding passage*

CONCLUSION

In this chapter, I introduced several prominent regional music genres and their musical characteristics. There are many more regional genres that deserve close examination. Regardless of the music or ensemble type, all of them have a distinct sound quality and character. These distinguishing musical features, either called regional flavor or color, are elements upon which a sense of local identity is built. From my observation, a regional music evokes a sense of emotional attachment for people from the region that no outsiders would experience. Although Chinese scholars continue to see regional music as part of a large category called national music, regional musics have maintained their own identities and have remained socially significant for the local people who practice and consume them.

Musical Interfaces between East and West

When Tan Dun (last name Tan) accepted the award for the best original score for Taiwanese director Ang Lee's 2000 motion picture *Crouching Tiger, Hidden Dragon,* he became the first Chinese composer ever to win an Oscar. Performed by the famous cellist Yo-yo Ma and several Chinese instrumentalists, the music was composed to accompany a story about Chinese martial arts. Utilizing musical gestures commonly found in Chinese music such as pentatonic scale, glissando, hetero- phonic texture, and timbre, Tan Dun creatively composed a score that matches the Chinese sceneries and sentiments evoked in the story. Winning this prestigious award not only further cemented Tan's career as a professional composer in the West but also rekindled global atten- tion toward Chinese music. Among his latest projects is a large-scale opera commissioned by the New York Metropolitan Opera based on the story of the first Chinese emperor Qin Shi Huang of the Qin dynasty (221–207 B.C.E.).

These recent events are evidence that the popularity of Chinese music beyond China is on the rise, although some would ask if these really are indeed examples of Chinese music. Recalling the historical interactions between Chinese and Western music reveals quite a dif- ferent picture. In the mid-nineteenth century, the French composer Hector Berlioz and the Gramophone Company's recording engineer F. W. Gaisberg described Chinese music as "likened to the sound of yowling cats" (Jones 2001: 19). Despite unfavorable reactions such as that one, the reception of Chinese music in the Western cultures has changed dramatically in recent years. At the same time, receptive to Western music, Chinese musicians have developed their own styles by strategically selecting elements from both cultural traditions. This chapter discusses the mutual influences between Chinese music and Western music. How has Chinese music been received in "the West,"

primarily Europe and North America? What changed as Chinese musicians began to incorporate practices of European and American music
into theirs? What kind of Chinese music is being produced in the
modern era, and how does recent global focus on Chineseness affect
Chinese music composition?

A GLIMPSE AT CHINESE MUSIC
IN EUROPE AND AMERICA

Information about Chinese music started to be brought back to Europe
through Jesuit missionaries and other travelers in the sixteenth century.
From the Chinese court at the end of sixteenth century, Italian Jesuit
priest Matteo Ricci (1552–1610) wrote accounts of various aspects of
Chinese culture, including music. In 1750, the French Jesuit missionary
Jean Joseph Amiot (1718–1793) went to China and subsequently took
extensive knowledge about Chinese language, science, and the arts back
to Europe. His fifteen-volume *Memoires concernant l'histoire, les sciences et
les arts des Chinois* (Paris, 1776–1791) contains some of the first comprehensive documentation and observations of Chinese music published in
the West. However, Amiot's report contains theoretical topics such as
instrumental classification and calculation of temperament rather than
notated music. Of the instruments he discusses, all were court instruments rather than those of the common people.

From the eighteenth century on, Chinese music gradually attracted
the attention of European composers, although their attitude toward
Chinese music was not always favorable. Like all non-European musics
of the time, Chinese music constituted a source of exotic sounds that
composers could use to "flavor" or "spice up" their music. Pieces with
Chinese themes began to appear starting with the work of eighteenth-
century French composer Jean-Philippe Rameau (1683–1764). During
the nineteenth century, compositions inspired by Chinese music began
to increase in number. Among the most famous works are the opera
*Turnandot w*ritten by Giacomo Puccini (1858–1924) and *Das Lied von
der Erde* (*The Song of the Earth*) by Gustav Mahler (1860–1911). The
stereotypical essentialized musical "formulas" ranged from the use of
pentatonic (five-pitch) scale, quasifolk melody, shrill vocal quality, and
quotes from ancient poems to evoking a sense of fantasy and myth.
All six movements of Mahler's symphonic song cycle *Das Lied von der
Erde,* for instance, employed translations of six Tang dynasty poems as
lyrics.

ACTIVITY 4.1 *Listen to CD track 33 and see whether you recognize any Chinese quality in the theme of Mahler's* Das Lied *movement 3. Take note of the tuning of any clearly presented musical "formulas" you hear in the music. How does the composer seem to intend to convey a sense of Chineseness in his music?*

Judging from Mahler's piece, it is clear that European composers had limited exposure to Chinese music and performance. What they learned about Chinese music was mostly from written sources rather than from direct contact with the music or musicians.

The situation for American composers was quite the contrary. The American familiarity with Chinese music came through immigration of Chinese to the New World. Massive migration of Chinese to the West Coast, Hawai'i, and New York in the nineteenth century had brought Chinese music and performers. In particular, Cantonese opera was frequently heard in Chinese communities in San Francisco, New York, and Honolulu because most of the immigrants were from Guangdong province. Although popular among audiences in the Chinese community, Cantonese opera was not always well received by audiences beyond the Chinese communities. In 1852, a Cantonese opera troupe, Tong Hook Tong Dramatic Company from Guangzhou, was contracted to perform in New York (Tchen 1999: 86). Unfortunately, the troupe failed to attract enough audience to survive because their music was too "foreign" for the local audience. In the 1930s in Honolulu, complaints were filed by local residents against the nightly Cantonese opera performance venues in and near Chinatown for noise disturbance. This finally led to a ban on performing opera after certain hours in the evening. [For more details on theatrical performances in nineteenth- and twentieth-century America, please refer to the excellent works on Chinese-American music by authors such as Krystyn Moon (2005).] Despite these social disturbances, the sound of Cantonese opera and music was no stranger to many Americans who resided in these cities. This opened a door for American composers who were exposed to and benefited directly from contact with Chinese music.

The reception of Cantonese opera may have been partially a result of racial prejudice. As newcomers and a minority in the United States, Chinese and other immigrant groups were subjected to ridicule and discrimination. In theatrical performances and freak shows, Chinese performers dressed in Chinese gowns frequently appeared as exotic spectacles to attract curious customers. Beginning in the 1880s, P. T. Barnum's display of the "Siamese Twins" Chang and Eng further reinforced the exotic perception of Chinese. Coupled with this stereotypical display of people were music compositions created to ridicule the Chinese. This was done by relying on existing musical and racial stereotype such as using pentatonic scales to construct melodies, excessive use of repeated notes in the motives, and the sound of the gong to represent Chineseness. These compositions presented a false impression of Chinese music as static and easily can be reduced to a set of stock musical gestures and formulas; this stands in stark contrast to the materials presented in the previous chapters.

Moon (2005) notes that the 1910 song "Chinatown, My Chinatown," written by William Jerome and Jean Schwartz, contains stereotypical elements that were found in much music that attempts to "sound Chinese" (102). One of these—heard in the main motive and made up of four repeated sixteenth-notes followed by two eighth-notes—remains one of the sonic signatures of Chineseness (CD track 34) and has even been used as a cellular ring tone. This trite portrayal of Chineseness also found its way into mainstream theatrical productions and movies. In other words, the Chinese flavors evoked here are based on fabrications and imagination of Chinese music rather than music practiced by insiders.

ACTIVITY 4.2 *Listen to CD track 34 and then to CD tracks 18 and 20. Compare the music in these examples to find any moments that dispute or support the stereotype of Chineseness. Take note of the timings of the moments in the tracks. To test the assumption of stereotypicality, it will be interesting to compare your examples to those of your classmates.*

The interaction of American composers with Chinese material intensified and deepened through the twentieth century. For example, Californian composer Lou Harrison (1917–2003), who was inspired by Chinese music, took instrumental instruction with musicians in San Francisco's Chinatown. For his *Music for Violin with Various Instruments* (1967), he built a zither whose playing techniques and timbre were modeled on the Chinese plucked zither *guzheng* (Figure 2.9) that you hear on CD track 20.

The attempt to present Chinese music in Western music has inevitably been entangled in the long history of presenting the Chinese as exotic others in Europe and in the United States. The methods by which composers incorporate Chinese music into compositions vary. Some composers quote a melody directly, some take a small segment of a piece and combine it with tonal harmony, and others create a new harmonic language based on the pentatonic scale. Some, armed with little knowledge of Chinese music, create work that is based on musical stereotypes, which Chinese-American composer Chou Wen-chung called "superficial borrowing." The popular cellular ring tone called "Asian Jingle" is a fine example of this kind of stereotype. Other examples of evoking a generic Chinese/Asian character are found in the music of many movies and musicals.

ACTIVITY 4.3 *If you want to deepen your awareness of musical essentializing, gather a few friends and rent the 1961 movie* Flower Drum Song, *the 1955 Disney animation production of* Lady *and the* Tramp, *or Disney's 1998* Mulan. *While watching, focus on the music. What musical means do you hear for suggesting an essentialized Chinese or Asian character? Is it by the use of the simplicity of the melody, the repeated notes, pentatonic melodies, or the singing style? If you or any friend knows the "Asian Jingle" cellular ring tone, think about it with the same question. Discuss this with your friends to see if you hear similarly.*

While Western composers are busy incorporating Chinese elements (imagined or otherwise) in their music, Chinese composers have been moving in the opposite direction. The process of adopting Western music has spawned a new way of thinking about music and has prompted Chinese composers to either fuse Western music with traditional sounds or turn their back on traditional Chinese music. As a result, Chinese music has gone through tremendous transformation. The West has gradually become more open to music of the others while Chinese composers have been Westernizing their music modeled on the perceptions that Western music equates with modernization. In chapter 2, I briefly mentioned the impact of Western music in China. A close look at how Chinese musicians have incorporated Western music is informative for understanding its recent development.

WESTERN MUSIC IN CHINA

Music of Europe was introduced into China via two major avenues. The first was through missionaries. Catholic missionaries arrived in China as early as the Yuan and Ming dynasties during the thirteenth and fifteenth centuries. Jesuit priests such as Mateo Ricci and others brought Western music to the Chinese court. This sort of introducing continued. During the seventeenth century, the Qing court hired Belgian priest Ferdinandus Verbiest (1623–1688) and Portuguese priest Thomas Pereira (1645–1708) as music teachers. Despite the presence of European musicians in China over a few centuries, the impact of their music in China was confined to the imperial court. Dissemination of Western music in a large scale occurred from the nineteenth century when Protestant missionaries from the United States and Britain arrived in large numbers across the country. In some respects, like the situation of Japan's process of adopting Western music (Wade 2004: 10), Western hymn singing began to circulate widely among the general public, indirectly promoting the popularity of tonal music.

Around the same time, students who studied in Japan and Europe at the beginning of the twentieth century began to bring back knowledge of Western music. This further helped to promote tonal music among the general public. As early as 1901, Chinese students were sent to study music in Japan. What they learned was a type of Euro-American music filtered through Japanese musical lenses. For example, one of the earliest students, Li Shutong (1880–1942), went to Japan in 1905 and returned to China with a type of hymnlike school song (see ibid.: 14). Tireless in promoting school songs, he also began to compose them.

As the European-inspired education system gradually replaced traditional Confucian learning, music was added to the curriculum as part of education for cultivating morality, civility, and ethics. Thus, music educators were crucial in disseminating tonal music in China through their published works (Figure 4.1). Ironically, the use of European music in modern education also reaffirms the Confucian teaching of emphasizing the role of music in the education of a learned person. I shall return to this in the next chapter.

Besides songs, Chinese musicians also began to perform Western instrumental music. The first military band was established in Beijing in 1920 by a British customs officer named Robert Hart (1835–1911). According to the Chinese music scholar Han Kuo Huang (1979), it was the first time that Chinese musicians were included to play alongside Western musicians. A chronicle of Shanghai music recorded that in the

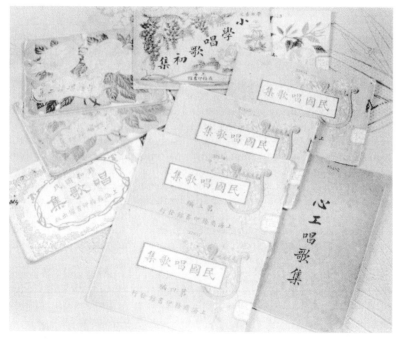

FIGURE 4.1   *Cover of a publication of song schools. (Courtesy of Yu Siuwah)*

port city of Shanghai, there were many formal and informal concert halls in the 1930s. Many Western orchestra and ensembles employed both local and foreign musicians for their nightly performance throughout the city. While the European classical music scene was in full swing, big band music for dances and cabarets were popular in China. Andrew Jones' (2001) account of American big bands and jazz musicians in Shanghai revealed the popularity of jazz and American tin-pan alley music in the city, which was nicknamed the "New York of the Orient."

In the face of increasing popularity of various types of international music through commercial gramophone recordings as well as other forms of modern entertainment, many traditionalists feared that traditional music would gradually disappear. In response to this perceived threat, they began to focus on promoting Chinese music as a way to counteract the encroachment of Western culture and music. But they did it in a "modernist" rather than preservationist sort of way. Many musicians experimented with new ways of composing music and modernizing traditional instruments. Some even went as far as restructuring traditional music according to Western sonic ideals and aesthetics—combining instruments for new ensemble types, modifying sounds of the instruments, and standardizing tuning systems and compositional procedures. Regardless of their success and intensity, these experiments laid an important foundation for the development of a modernist vision for traditional Chinese music.

It was at that time that regional musicians began to adopt the term *national music* to characterize their music. In the 1930s and 1940s, quite a few Cantonese and *jiangnan sizhu* musicians began to refer to their musics as *guoyue* (national music). While we will never know the real reasons why they chose the term we do know it communicates two different meanings. It was used to differentiate Chinese music from Western music, and it was used to position alongside Western-influenced music a subset of a large entity called national music. Clearly, the label designates a more open-ended rather than restrictive definition of *guoyue* than some conservative musicians had been advocating (see chapter 3).

Despite the prevention efforts proposed by different musicians, it was clear that much of traditional Chinese music had been affected by certain European musical ideals. This included the use of printed music, the standardization of the score and tuning, and the changing performance venues for traditional music. Although there were isolated efforts proposed to preserve traditional music, the establishment of conservatories and the government promotion of European music inevitably reduced its popularity especially among the urban youth. While traditional music continued to be performed intermittently in public venues such as teahouses, at social functions, and during religious events, more and more Chinese music events began to be performed on stage in modern concert halls and theaters. This changing performance setting signified a major departure from traditional musical practices and social functions of music.

Piano in China.   In 1999, Chinese-born pianist Lang Lang rocked the concert world with his dazzling performance with the Chicago Symphony as a last-minute substitution (Figure 4.2). Soon afterward, his concert career skyrocketed and now he performs in major concert venues around the world. Trained in China as well as the United States, he is the first Chinese pianist to be engaged by major orchestras in the world. Adding to his illustrious performance career was his appointment as UN Goodwill Ambassador in 2004. Success stories like this are not unusual nowadays considering the large number Chinese pianists winning major international competitions and studying in major

FIGURE 4.2   *A piano child prodigy born and raised in Shenyang province, Lang Lang won the Shenyang Piano Competition at the age of five. In 1995, at thirteen years of age, he won first prize at the Tchaikovsky International Young Musicians' Competition in Japan. In 1997, he began his music studies at the Curtis Institute in Philadelphia. His professional career began in 1999 after his Chicago performance. Lang Lang has won numerous awards and has performed with major orchestras throughout the world. He was recently recognized by the UN Children's Fund for his work on youth and music; the UN appointed him their 2004 international Goodwill Ambassador. (Courtesy of www.langlangfans.org)*

conservatories in the United States and Europe. So why are so many Chinese attracted to the piano?

Among the Western instruments imported into China, the piano seems to have had the most appeal not only for musicians but also for the general public. Unlike in Japan, in China the adoption of Western music was not a full-scale project coordinated by the government. Rather, the influence of the individual musicians and music educators impacted its reception. For instance, early music educators Sheng Xinggong (1870–1947), Li Shutong (1880–1942), and Xiao Youmei (1884–1940) all studied piano and considered it an important foundation for learning Western music. This attitude toward the piano greatly enhanced its popularity. Its acceptance among the emerging middle class of the time also explained why most music educational programs in the 1920s and 1930s created large piano divisions in newly formed music departments and programs (see chapter 2).

As an icon of European music, the piano was received in China as more than a musical instrument. Because of its construction, tuning system, well-defined repertory and pedagogy, and international appeal, the piano was perceived as a manifestation of European scientific superiority (Kraus 1989). Playing the piano was a way of being modern and participating in the advanced fine arts of Europe. The piano was to become an essential symbol of high social status for most middle-class families, very like its status in nineteenth-century Europe.

With this demand, piano importers and musical instrument factories began to flood the local market. One of the earliest companies to import musical instruments to China was the English firm Moutrie; a branch in China was established in 1843. Initially specializing in importing pump organs, the company switched to producing pianos in Shanghai. In 1920s an average of over one hundred pianos were made there every month. Another British company, Robinson, also established a branch in Shanghai in 1875 to import printed music and musical instruments of famous makers such as Steinway, Bechstein, and Bluthner. Besides these high-end products, local Chinese piano companies also began to produce relatively inexpensive instruments to meet the market demand. The earliest Chinese-owned piano factory was Xiang Xing Piano Company, established in 1890 in Shanghai.

With the rising popularity of the piano, Chinese composers found a new outlet for their creativity. Many piano pieces based on Chinese themes were written. Although the Chinese practice of writing new music based on old tunes had long been established in tradition, fitting a Chinese melody with European-style accompaniment became a challenge for many composers. One of the Chinese piano compositions that gained international recognition was a piece called "A Shepherd's Flute" written in 1934 by He Luting (1903–1999) (CD track 35). The story of how this piece came to be known internationally is interesting because it reveals another significant factor in the modernizing of Chinese composition: the active role of Western musicians in China.

Since the 1920s, Shanghai has been a cosmopolitan center and a cultural hub in Asia. Like the importance of present-day New York City and London for the arts, Shanghai emerged as China's premier cultural center where new trends in the arts have been developed and launched. Many Western musicians and artists have traveled to Shanghai to lecture and give performances, contributing significantly to the flourishing arts scene. Among them was a Russian composer named Alexander Tcherepnin (1899–1977) (Figure 4.3).

FIGURE 4.3   *Picture of Alexander Tcherepnin (1899– 1977). (Courtesy of The Tcherepnin Society)*

Tcherepnin was born into a musical family on January 21, 1899, in St. Petersburg, Russia. His father was active as a composer and performer in Russia and Europe in the early 1930s and as a composition professor at the St. Petersburg Conservatory, where young Alexander studied at the age of eighteen. As a pianist, Alexander embarked on a worldwide concert tour that took him to Asia. During this trip, he became interested in Chinese and Japanese folk songs. His *Five "Chinese" Concert Etudes* for piano (1934–1936), *Piano Method on Pentatonic Scale* (1934), and *No. 3 Bagatelles Chinoises* (*Chinese Bagatelles*) (1935) were all composed during his China days and pioneered the style of modern Chinese piano pieces. Deeply attracted by Chinese music, Tcherepnin canceled the rest of his tour and remained in China. While in China, he performed in Shanghai at the National Conservatory (see chapter 2) and later lived there for a period of time. A large number of composition students at the National Conservatory studied with him and he worked closely with many Chinese musicians. He devoted himself to educating Chinese composers to express their native style by integrating native elements with Western music. The young He Luting was one of his composition students there.

One of the most influential twentieth-century Chinese composers and music educators, He Luting (1903–1999) was born into a poor family in central China. After graduating from high school, he was accepted into one of the newly established local academies of art. In 1933, he was admitted to the National Conservatory of Music majoring in composition. In Shanghai he was exposed to many different types of music and to political thinking. "Mutong duandi" ("A Shepherd's Flute," CD track 35) is a piano work that He Luting wrote for the composition competition sponsored by Alexander Tcherepnin in Shanghai in 1934. This unique competition was established by Tcherepnin to encourage the publication and dissemination of new works composed in the Chinese style. He Luting's career flourished after the winning the competition, and he continued to compose pieces that incorporated Chinese elements as a basis. He is known as one of the most important modern Chinese composers.

ACTIVITY 4.4   *"Mutong duandi" is a short piano piece written in a three-part ABA form (CD track 35). First listen to CD track 35 in its entirety. After that, pay close attention to the different sections. The first part "A" (to 1:07) is made up*

of a lyrical melody. It is set to the now-familiar five-note scale that can be easily heard by playing consecutive black keys on the piano. The "B" part (1:07–1:32), starting after a slight pause, is different in character with the lefthand part changed to a chordal accompaniment while the right hand plays a melody made up of a triplet figure. The initial "A" section returns at 1:33 but with a more complicated part played in a lower register.

Listen carefully to the use of the melodic motive throughout the piece. Is the melody in the upper register or in the bass? Describe the activity of the righthand and lefthand part in the "A" section of the piece and contrast it to that of the section "B." Consider whether or not this music sounds "Chinese" to you. If so, why? If not, why not?

Since He Luting's time, the piano has continued to play an important role in Chinese music. In the 1940s, many Chinese composers were writing music for the piano, but most of them were writing in the style that was similar to the work spearheaded by He Luting and his contemporaries. During the Cultural Revolution (1967–1977), while most Western instruments were banned, the piano was one of the few instruments allowed to be used in the Revolutionary Peking Opera, also called "Model opera." I will return to the Cultural Revolution and "Model opera" in the next chapter.

NEW VOICES IN CHINESE MUSIC

The music discussed thus far, understood as embracing Western music aesthetics, practice, and sensibility, is modern Chinese music. Most people consider the period around the May 4th Movement in 1919, the student-led protest calling for the abolition of old and traditional learning in favor of new and Western sciences, to be the beginning of modern Chinese music. The term *modern,* which did not exist in the Chinese language, was adopted from the beginning of the twentieth century in the phonetic equivalent of *modang* and was given Chinese characters. To be "modern" in the Chinese context implies being up-to-date, new, unconventional, and Westernized. The Chinese for modern music, *xiandai yinyue,* refers primarily to music written for Western instruments, which includes anything from concert music to popular music.

Since the early days of the twentieth century, Chinese music has continued to transform as it absorbs many outside influences. After World War II (1939–1945) and with the increasing migration of Chinese people globally, the new modern Chinese music took forms quite different from the styles attempted by earlier composers. While Chinese composers in China were composing music with strong political messages, those who were living outside China were continuing their efforts to find a new voice for their music.

Chou Wen-chung. One of the most important of the composers who have lived their creative lives outside of China is Chou Wen-chung (Figure 4.4). Chou was born in Yentai in Shandong province, China, in 1923. Like many other Chinese students who studied engineering at the time, Chou came to the United States right in 1946 to study architecture at Yale, one of the few U.S. universities that had established academic affiliations with Chinese universities. His fascination with music eventually took him to the New England Conservatory and to Columbia University, where he studied composition with the famous French-turned-American composer Edgar Varèse (1883–1965). Despite the fact that his compositions are based on the avant-garde music idiom, his work and composition ideals are also based on traditional Chinese music.

Chou Wen-chung advocates "a remerger of Eastern and Western musical concepts and practices" (Chou 1969). With a very long view of history, in his opinion, the two traditions once shared the same origin and inspiration but each took on unique characteristics because of their respective cultural contexts. To Chou, the question of creating modern Chinese music and merging the East and West requires a process of cross-pollination that "transcends cultural colonialism and chauvinism."

In his influential 1970s essay "Asian Concepts and Twentieth-Century Western Composers," Chou draws parallels between Chinese music and that of two twentieth-century music giants—Edgar Varèse and Anton Webern. He claims that "Varèse's concept of music as "organized sound" and of sound as "living matter" is a modern Western parallel of a pervasive Chinese concept: that each single tone is a musical entity in itself, that musical meaning is intrinsic in the tones themselves (1971: 215–216). Chou is convinced that his music, although modernist and avant-garde in outlook, is steeped in classical Chinese philosophy

FIGURE 4.4   *Composer Chou Wen-chung at the Society for Ethnomusicology meeting in Atlanta. 2005. (Courtesy of Frederick Lau)*

and embraces the Chinese literati *wenren* impulse of leadership, culturalism, and vision.

On principle, Chou warns Chinese musicians against blindly following Western style. In a speech he gave in 2004, he remarked:

"A composition based on the adoption of Western concepts, techniques and styles but embellished with Asian effects and color, even when composed by a Chinese or Asian, remains a product of emulation. Because such music is not a crystallization of cultural interaction, it is incapable of asserting itself as intercultural contemporary music. Frankly, the development of Chinese music still awaits efforts that are more profound in depth and in breadth. To truly point to the future, the work will have to reveal the intrinsic values of both worlds. And it will have to demonstrate a degree of synthesis in ideas, skills, and expression. Only then can we arrive at an ideal stage-one that every sincere artist or composer should aspire to. What is worrisome is the convention of idolizing the West, pursuing trendy fashion, and indulging in fame and vanity. Let us hope these distractions will dissipate with time." (quoted in Pan-Chew 2004: 118)

Chou's ideals for developing China's modern music are rather different from those of his predecessors. His perspective is almost a complete opposite of what earlier Chinese composers were doing—writing Chinese-"flavored" music by framing a Chinese melody in a Western form. That is, Chou's works are mostly based on the underlying principles and essence of Chinese music rather than simply borrowing the superficial elements like a pentatonic scale or folk song melody. His vision of advancing Chinese modern music and breaking from the established ways of utilizing Chinese materials in new ways can be seen in his 1965 chamber composition "Yu ko" (CD track 36).

"Yu ko," a fisherman's song (1965), was written for violin, wind instruments, piano, and percussion. This piece was derived from an old *guqin* piece that carries the same title. In the music, Chou retains the original programmatic reference of the *guqin* piece. The music evokes the serenity of man in harmony with nature. By imitating the subtle playing techniques of the *guqin* (CD track 37) on modern instruments, Chou created a piece whose characteristics are founded on manipulating musical parameters such as microtonal pitch bending, articulations, changing timbre, dynamics, and flexible rhythm. Chou's emphasis on the subtlety of *guqin* music also highlights his preference for the deep rootedness of Chinese music (see chapter 5). He believes that any new music should be derived from a thorough understanding of a long tradition. As stated in an interview, Chou is strongly against selling out and compromising one's music to suit popular taste and market value:

"Unfortunately at the moment, the arts in the United States have been completely taken over by giant corporations and converted into commodities for entertainment. It has become fashionable to adopt the so-called 'non-Western' aura or to display the so-called 'mystic' philosophy or religious catchwords of the West to intoxicate the public with little understanding of Asian cultures. Even worse is to ignorantly apply and distort the essences of Eastern cultures under the banner of cultural exchange. Whereas, on the other hand, composers who are not yet controlled by the entertainment industry are ignored entirely. All of these could be recognized by composers and educators elsewhere so as to maintain one's own 'independent' spirit, thereby avoiding the pitfall of blind emulation of imitation, or worse, being manipulated as merchandise." (quoted in Pan-Chew 2004: 120)

ACTIVITY 4.5 *In his composition "Yu ko," Chou attempts to transmit the essence of* guqin *music through the use of various Western instruments. Listen to CD track 36 and compare what you hear there to CD track 37. Do you hear any of the details beyond the pitch bending, timbral change, sudden dynamic change, and metric change? Make a listening chart for CD track 37 plotting the musical elements you can identify.*

"New Wave" Composers. The development of Chinese modern music reached new heights after the fall of the Gang of Four in the late 1970s. During what was known as the Cultural Revolution (1966–1976), the Gang of Four advocated extremely fundamentalist thoughts and banned selected Western and traditional Chinese instruments (*guqin*, for instance) and practices. They selected what they considered as "modern" and acceptable. Their downfall brought a new age of cultural and economic freedom to China that started in the early 1980s and continues today. Under the influence of an open-door policy, artists have emerged and revitalized the modernist trend that had been temporarily halted for political reasons.

In music, the modernists adopted avant-garde music and the practice of atonal music instead of the more conventional political music that had been promoted in the 1950s. A group of Central Conservatory (Beijing) compositions students who shared a common experience of having been sent to work in the countryside during the Cultural Revolution began to compose pieces in a style that was considered new and avant-garde. Influenced by visiting composers such as Alexander Goehr, George Crumb, Chou Wen-chung, and others, these students began to explore new ways of expanding the conventions of music-writing in China.

Because of their avant-garde musical thinking, this group of composers was called the "New Wave" or "New Tide." Tan Dun, the composer of the score for the film *Crouching Tiger, Hidden Dragon,* and a few other composers such as Chen Yi, Zhou Long, Bright Sheng, and Ge Ganru were among the most prominent composers of this group.

Chou Wen-chung's teaching was particularly influential among them because several of them left China in 1986 and 1987 to study with Chou at Columbia University. At present, all of them have established their careers in the United States and are enjoying tremendous success in the international new music scene. Among members of the "New Wave" composers, Tan Dun seems to have attracted the most public attention because of his involvement in the film industry. His work is multi-dimensional in style and incorporates many different musical idioms. However, the central component of his style is derived from concepts of sound drawn from Chinese music.

Tan Dun was born in 1957 in Hunan, central China, and was raised in a rural area. His official biography mysteriously states that he grew up in a land "filled with magic, ritual, and shamanism." Sent to plant rice on a commune during the Cultural Revolution, Tan was later assigned to play *erhu* with the provincial *jingju* Beijing Opera Company. His extensive knowledge of music, in particular local folk songs, led him to be accepted to the Beijing Central Conservatory in 1978, where he studied classical Western composition. There he was joined by a group of young composers experimenting with various avant-garde techniques. Tan intertwined the aesthetic of traditional Chinese music and the mysterious shaman ritual sounds of his childhood in remarkable compositions. In 1986, he received a fellowship to study at Columbia University, where he studied composition with Chou Wen-chung. He struggled to reconcile his creative impulses with the Western avant-garde style in order to establish a personal style that incorporates both Chinese music and innovation.

An example of Tan's conscious blending of Chinese musical elements in his music can be heard in his *Ghost Opera for String Quartet and Pipa* (1994, CD track 38). This is a piece he wrote after moving to New York, where he came under the influence of many musical styles and idioms. In this piece, he superimposes European language with Chinese folk song, sentiments, and the ancient tradition of "ghost opera." To create a contrast to the atonal language, he balanced it by using the Chinese plucked lute *pipa* with its characteristics tremolos, glissandos, microtonal pitch bending, and melodic figurations (CD track 4). These references to traditional Chinese music and the use of Chinese instruments seem to be a standard approach for Tan and the New Wave composers.

Another common practice among these composers is the incorporation of traditional instruments into the Western idiom. For the film score of *Crouching Tiger, Hidden Dragon,* Tan Dun effectively combined

Chinese and Western instruments. The practice of creating a music based on Western music idiom with strong Chinese characteristics is evident in his chamber piece "Double Watchtower" ("Shuang Que") (CD track 39) for *erhu* and *yangqin*. In this piece, Tan begins with a solo *erhu* melody written in a traditional pentatonic scale. The *yangqin* (CD track 7) gradually appears in the background as an accompaniment before emerging as the solo instrument. The musical idiom for the accompaniment is set in an atonal musical language that creates moments of interjection into the serene pentatonic Chinese melody. Other interesting features of this piece are the use of quiet and slow passages in the first part of the piece to contrast the fast and rhythmic section that dominates the latter half.

ACTIVITY 4.6   *Listen to CD track 35 carefully and follow the events given in the guide.*

Section A

0:00–0:30	*Solo pentatonic* erhu *melody, slow, sparse, and orna-mented with glissando*
0:31–1:27	Yangqin *enters, playing passages without a tonal center*
1:28–1:35	Erhu *strings being plucked*
1:36–1:59	*New* yangqin, *new accompaniment pattern*
2:10–2:15	*Silence*
2:21	Erhu *tune reappears with a tonal accompaniment*
3:07–3:39	Erhu *solo*

Section B

3:43	*Fast section begins with fast-moving repeated notes on the* yangqin
4:45	*Passage without a tonal center*
4:15	*New accompaniment emerges*
5:17	Erhu *playing double stops—two strings at the same time*

Section C

5:46	*New sound emerges*

> 6:12   *More* erhu *double stops*
> 6:20–7:23   *Fast-moving repeated notes with the melody played by the* erhu
>
> • *The music at 3:07–3:19 takes on a different character. Describe what you hear in terms of the melody and the use of the* erhu.
> • *What creates the new sound at 5:46?*
> • *How does the* erhu *theme compare to the music of Abing heard on CD track 18?*

"Double Watchtower" ("Shuang que") contains many of Tan Dun's later compositional techniques—a deliberate fusion and juxtaposition of both Western and Chinese elements from past and present. According to Tan Dun, despite his strong reference to Chinese music, his musical practice is no longer about China. The "Asian" sounds in this music are not part of an artificial attempt to proclaim Chineseness. Instead he asserts that they are a natural means of expression; for him, this kind of musical fusion is not about being traditional, national, or international. It is simply about being human. Music is for and about people.

> **ACTIVITY 4.7**   *Select one of these composers as a topic: Chen Yi, Zhou Long, Bright Sheng, and Ge Ganru. Listen to the composer's music if you have access to it, but in any case investigate and write a paper about the composer's career path and compositions. Based on your findings on compositional strategies and aesthetics, does your composer's work conform to Chou's comments (given earlier) about modern compositions?*

POPULAR MUSIC

Chinese popular music, generally known as *liuxing yinyue* or *liuxing gequ* ("popular songs"), has a relatively short but vibrant history in China. Emerging in the 1920s, *liuxing yinyue* was China's response to imported, modern, Western, and in particular, American popular music.

It was music created for an emerging urban population and for mass consumption. Modeled on the musical style of Hollywood films, the music was closely linked to the Chinese movie and recording industry of the time. This popular entertainment form incorporated elements of traditional Chinese music but transformed them into one unique genre.

While the early Chinese popular music *liuxing yinyue* was modeled on big band jazz style, its melodies were based on pentatonic scales with lyrics sung in Mandarin Chinese (CD track 40). It was performed mostly in dance halls, nightclubs, and movies and as part of song and dance shows. Shanghai, the most cosmopolitan city of China, became the center of this new entertainment form. Foreign gramophone companies such as Pathe, EMI, and RCA-Victor set up recording studios in the city since the 1920s, producing 78 rpm vinyl recordings for local and regional consumption (Jones 2001). Because of the popularity of Chinese popular music across the country of the time, it essentially became another kind of "national music" that transcends regional association and identification.

Mandarin popular songs are considered by scholars to be the first kind of modern popular music developed in China. Developed in Shanghai in the 1920s and mostly associated with movies, their musical features became standardized and widely distributed as the record industry began to flourish in Hong Kong and Taiwan because of political instability in China (ibid.). Mandarin was originally the local dialect of Beijing, but it rose to prominence as the Chinese national language in the early twentieth century. Since then, it has been considered the language of the modern, educated class throughout China.

Because the content of these early popular songs was about romance, love, and, by implication, the decadence of urban life, some considered them harmful to society and nicknamed this kind of song "pornographic" music or *yellow* music. It is important to remember in this regard that in Confucianist thought, music has the power to affect people's morale and behavior.

Among the most prolific songwriters of the time was Li Jinhui (1891–1967), who wrote many hit songs. Interestingly, Li was also a member of Liu Tianhua's Association of National Music Research (Guoyue Yanjiuhui) playing silk and bamboo music (see chapter 2), and his Western music training was minimal. During the 1920s, he wrote children's music and in the 1930 began to compose film music. He was also famous for his role in writing music for the New Moon Songs and Dance troupe, a women's music and dance group whose popularity spread beyond Shanghai to Hong Kong and Southeast Asia. He collaborated with many

FIGURE 4.5 *The famous 1930s Shanghai popular singer and actress Zhou Xuan. (Courtesy of Frederick Lau)*

singer/actresses of the time. Among them were Zhou Xuan (Figure 4.5), the female singer nicknamed "the golden voice" of Shanghai-style popular songs. Both Li and Zhou were pivotal figures in the early history of Chinese popular music. Their collaboration further promoted Zhou's legendary career, which was ended by her suicide at age thirty-four.

Shanghai-style popular songs dominated the Chinese popular music market until the 1950s when a significant part of the movie and recording industry moved to British-colonial Hong Kong. This was an effect of the Chinese Communist Party gaining complete political control of China in 1949. The production of pop songs in China halted, to be replaced by revolutionary music and songs laden with political propaganda.

Notions of popular music shifted to songs with strong anti-Western imperialist messages written to glorify the Communist Party.

In Hong Kong and Taiwan the production of Shanghai-style popular songs called *shidaiqu* ("songs of the epoch") continued. The word *Mandarin* was added to distinguish them from a similar type of popular song sung in other regional dialects such as Cantonese or Fujianese. In Hong Kong, the production and circulation of *shidaiqu* also indirectly stimulated the birth of a local popular music style called *Cantonese popular songs,* later known as *cantopop.*

Hong Kong Cantopop. *Cantopop,* a phenomenon that emerged during the 1970s, refers to a style of Hong Kong popular songs that are sung in Cantonese. It has dominated the Hong Kong music industry since the 1980s. Although Cantonese songs have been popular in Hong Kong since the 1930s, they are mostly associated with Cantonese narrative genres and opera (see chapter 3). *Cantopop,* however, is different from Cantonese opera in sound quality and musical style because it is inspired by Western "folk rock" music of the 1970s (e.g., the Carpenters, Bee Gees, and John Denver). *Cantopop* utilizes a rock band setup as accompaniments with ample use of electronic instruments such as electric guitar and synthesizer. Even with the use of Cantonese language and occasional use of selected Chinese instruments, the sound of *cantopop* has a special quality that makes it different from traditional Cantonese music. The singing style is lyrical in quality, similar to Western soft rock and Japanese popular songs. The lyrics are vernacular, colloquial, and contemporary in content, appealing to urban youth.

CD track 41 is a representative example of *cantopop* written by one of the pioneers of the genre, Sam Hui Koon-kit. Starting out his career by imitating the Beatles and singing Western cover songs, Hui gradually turned to singing and writing songs in Cantonese in the mid-1970s and produced his first *cantopop* album in 1978. In this ballad, "Langzhi hui tou" ("Vagabond's Desires"), originally written for the 1976 Cantonese movie *The Private Eyes,* Hui departed from his usual rock style and utilized instead an American folk song style and soft electronic sound to accompany his singing. Like many of Hui's songs about life and the struggle of working-class commoners, "Langzhi hui tou" advises listeners of the danger of vanity and encourages them to seek happiness by working hard and being realistic.

The overwhelming success of *cantopop* owes much to the popularity of TV serial drama in the 1980s, when most serial dramas were associated with a theme song. The prolific Shanghai-born song writer and band leader Joseph Koo, whose sister was a popular film star in Shanghai before 1949, was credited with writing many of what are now considered classic *cantopop* songs. Many *cantopop* singers localized Western and Japanese classics by rearranging the music and singing them in Cantonese, giving *cantopop* its unique quality and sonic identity. The 1980s and 1990s saw new developments in terms of diversification of styles and lyrics. During this period, the lyrics and musical style tended to be more local and political as the handover of Hong Kong was drawing near. In the new millennium, while *cantopop* has been reaching audiences throughout Asia, a new Chinese pop music scene also began to emerge in the PRC.

ACTIVITY 4.8 *The* cantopop *scene in Hong Kong has produced many superstars. In the 1990s, the four most prominent male superstars—Jackie Cheung, Andy Lau, Leon Lai, and Aaron Kwok—were coined the "Four Heavenly Kings." Try to locate a sound clip from any of their performances on the Internet. Then compare it to the early Chinese pop from Shanghai (CD track 40). Discuss the differences in singing style, voice quality, and accompaniment.*

The economic development of the 1980s in China once again transformed the popular music scene. The resurgence of lyrical popular songs in the early 1980s signified a remarkable change in music that had been dominated by political slogans and messages. In the early 1980s, Hong Kong and Taiwan style popular songs began to circulate in China. This was the music I heard on the street when I first visited Chaozhou. The most popular singer of the time in China was Teresa Teng, or Deng Lijun (1953–1995, Figure 4.6), who is well known for her crooning singing style (CD track 42). Teng, a Taiwan-born female singer, is considered the most celebrated transnational Chinese pop star of the 1970s and 1980s in China, Hong Kong, and Taiwan. This statement, made by songwriter Jia Ding, is a moving testimony that shows the tremendous impact of Teng's music, which can be extended to all pop songs from Hong Kong and Taiwan:

"The first time I heard Deng Lijun's songs was in 1978. I just stood there listening for a whole afternoon. I never knew before that the world had such good music. I felt such pain. I cried. I was really very excited and touched, and suddenly realized that my work in the past had no emotional force." (quoted in Jones 1992: 16)

FIGURE 4.6   *Teresa Teng. (Courtesy of Frederick Lau)*

The effect of Teng's music on mainland listeners is revealing because her popularity signified a shift in the communist policy of arts created by the economic reform of the late 1970s. Since that time, artistic expressions are no longer created only to serve the party and revolution but rather to express individual emotions and sentiments. The influx of Hong Kong and Taiwan popular songs also inspired the beginning of local popular music styles. Because of the relaxed political environment brought on by the open-door economic policy, a popular music market and recording industry began to reappear in China after forty years of inactivity. A number of styles of popular songs became available across the country and sparked discussions of the impact of popular music on society in the official media.

The term *tongsu gequ* ("popularized songs") began to gain currency but mostly referred to songs that were sanctioned and supported by government-run performing troupes. These songs range from lyrical to energetic or masculine with lots of shouts and harsh vocal timbre (Jones 1992: 23) and the content was often patriotic in tone and supportive of the nation. Despite a lyrical musical style and a break from the revolutionary song style of the earlier period, *tongsu gequ* were considered acceptable by the government because they were about collective emotion and glorification of the motherland. As a genre supported by the government, *tongsu gequ* are disseminated in state-run media such as television, radio, recording, and film.

Outside the official realm, many youngsters began to experiment with Anglo-American-style rock music, called *yaogun yinyue* (literally, "rock and roll"). Different from the state-supported musicians, rock musicians emphasize their inner emotions, struggles between reality and self-expression, and individualism and make a tacit commentary on current society. Their music, drastically different from the lyrical quality of "popularized songs" (*tongsu gequ*), is a direct copy of Western hard rock, punk rock, and heavy metal. Listening to some of these songs, one cannot help but be surprised how different these songs are from other Chinese contemporary popular songs that are close to the Western soft or folk rock style. Rock music circles consist of tight-knit social groups made up mostly of teenagers or people in their twenties. Unlike officially supported performing groups, they perform for private collective "parties" and in underground venues and dance clubs.

The pioneer of Chinese rock music is Cui Jian (last name Cui). Cui, a Chinese of Korean ancestry, was trained as a trumpet player at the famous Beijing Central Conservatory of Music. He performed with the Beijing Philharmonic Orchestra for several years until he was fired for performing his own compositions that criticized the government. With financial help from private companies and rock music instruction from foreign students and contacts, Cui Jian launched his own music career by performing with his rock band on university campuses. His first concert took place at Peking University, featuring a Madagascaran guitarist and a Hungarian guitarist (Jones 1992: 93). In 1986, Cui Jian stunned the music world by performing his by-now classic hit "I Have Nothing" ("Yiwu suoyou," CD track 43). In this piece he employs the characteristic sounds of rock but also creatively incorporates a solo played by the double-reed *suona* instead of the typical distorted sound of the guitar. The lyrics, written in Chinese, were sung with a coarse timbre common in rock music.

"I Have Nothing"	"Yiwu suoyou"
I have asked you repeatedly, when will you go with me?	Wo cengjing wenge buxiu, ni heshi gen wo zou
But you just always laugh at my having nothing	Keni que zong shi xiaowo, yiwu suoyou

I have given you my dreams, given you my freedom	woyao geini wode zhuiqiu, haishi wode zhiyou
But you always just laugh at my having nothing	Keni que zong shi xiaowo, yiwu suoyou
Oh! When will you go with me?	Oh! Ni heshi gen wo zou?
Oh! When will you go with me?	Oh! Ni heshi gen wo zou?
The earth under my feet is on the move	Jiaoxia zhedi zaizou
The water by my side is flowing on	Shenbian nashui zailiu
But you always just laugh at my having nothing	Keni que zong shi xiaowo, yiwu suoyou
Why haven't you laughed your fill?	Weihe ne zongxiaoge bugou?
Why will I always search?	Weihe wozongyao zhuiqiu
Could it be that before you I will always have nothing?	Nandao zaini qianmian, wo yongyuan shi, yiwu suoyou
Oh! When will you go with me?	Oh! Ni heshi gen wo zou?
Oh! When will you go with me?	Oh! Ni heshi gen wo zou?

Cui Jian's music was widely played during the student movements of the 1990s as a symbol of defiance and rebellion. Named the pioneer of modern Chinese rock music, he started a trend that has become the model for many rock bands since the 1990s. At present, China's rock scene continues to thrive in urban centers such as Beijing, Shanghai, and Guangzhou. Although it is far from being accepted by the mainstream, rock music is still a genre that occupies a niche market for urban youth. With the emergence of disco and clubs, rock music has created an audience and an outlet for many of China's next generation of rock musicians.

ACTIVITY 4.9 *Listen to the singing style on CD track 43 and compare it to the singing style of Zhou Xuan (CD track 40) and Teresa Teng (CD track 42). Write a description of the qualities of the voices and the singing styles. Also articulate how the accompaniments differ from one another.*

Minority Pop in the Mainstream.   Coupled with the government policy on ethnic minorities, the use of popular music opened the door to popular music of peoples other than the Han. The rise of Chinese popular music in the 1980s also spawned a new style of songs that centered on ethnic minority themes and images. Since the establishment of the PRC, the central government has recognized fifty-six ethnic groups as official minority nationalities. According to the 1949 minority autonomous laws, these minority groups have the right to maintain and develop their own cultures. Politically, however, they are under the control of the central government, which is dominated by the Han majority. This policy further reinforces the commonly held perception that the Han are civilized and that their culture is superior to that of the minorities. In the last few decades, however, ethnic minorities have attracted much attention because of the government's policy of encouraging ethnic pride and identity in order to portray China as a multi-ethnic unified nation. Songs and images of minorities are common in the state-run media and on television.

Minority music stereotypes have existed in China since the 1950s, for instance, a widespread impression of Mongolian singing as being characterized by free melismatic phrases in slow tempo accompanied by the horse-head bowed lute. The music of minorities in Xinjiang province in northwest China is represented in music by many Han and other composers by Middle Eastern sounding melodies and meters such as 5/8 or 7/8.

But recent minority pop music has taken on different meanings because of the changing social and cultural conditions associated with China's global connections, free-market economy, and a more relaxed political environment. In this new social setting, minority pop songs produced by native singers are immensely popular throughout the country. When I visited a CD store in southern China, the storefront was lined with minority pop by numerous Mongolian and Tibetan singers. The owner told me that this is the most popular music in the country. Teng Ge'er, Han Hong, Lolo, and Shan Ying are among some of the most popular singers of this genre. The reasons for their popularity reflect a changing attitude toward national minorities.

Teng Ge'er was born in 1960 in the Inner Mongolia Autonomous Region of China, where he studied *sanxian* at the Inner Mongolia Academy of Arts (Figure 4.7). Inner Mongolia, which borders several northern provinces in China such as Hebei and Shanxi, was recognized by the PRC government as an autonomous region in 1947. Its language and culture combine influences from both Mongolian and Chinese. However, the Republic of Mongolia, located north of Inner Mongolia, is a sovereign state that gained independence in 1924 from the Soviet socialist government. Raised in Inner Mongolia, Teng Ge'er studied Chinese-style composition and conducting at the China Conservatory in

FIGURE 4.7   *Teng Ge'er. (Courtesy of Frederick Lau)*

Beijing and Tianjin Conservatory. After graduation, he was employed as a performer in the Central Nationality Song and Dance Troupe. His career in popular music began after he won the first prize at the 1989 National Popular Music Singing Contest sponsored by the government. The following year, he also won a top prize at the International Popular Music competition held in the capital of the Republic of Mongolia, Ulan Bator. His music combines the Mongolian singing style with modern electronic sounds, often articulating a strong sense of nostalgia about being Mongolian. To achieve a Mongolian sentiment, he uses characteristic Mongolian sounds such as the horse-head bowed lute, Mongolian melodic material, and singing style to invoke elements of Mongolian culture such as grassland, horses, and a nomadic way of life. These musical features are represented in the song "Menggu Ren" ("The Mongols," CD track 44). This 1989 song, which describes the pride of being Mongolian and celebrates the role of the grassland in nurturing the Mongolian lifestyle, is a good example of how ethnic minorities and their identities are articulated sonically. According to Nimrod Baranovich's (2003) study of minority popular songs, the lyrics of the song "The Mongols" "not only omit the state, but also react against it and its assertions of control" (78). In the song, you first hear the melody sung in a slow tempo that is typical in Mongolian music, followed by a solo passage of the horse-head bowed lute. The lyrics speak of the Mongolian culture and countryside: "Smoke of cooking rises from the clean white yurt, in a herder's home where I was born, the vast and borderless grassland is the cradle that nurtures us....This is what a Mongolian is all about." Teng Ge'er once claimed, "If listeners can realize from my singing my intense love for the land and my sincerity towards life, it is because I am a Mongolian" (http://www.mtvtop.net/asp/dangan1.asp?name=%CC%DA%B8%F1%B6%FB). "The Mongols" was popular not only in Inner Mongolia but also in the Republic of Mongolia. Teng Ge'er's song symbolically creates a bond between Mongolians on both sides of the border and refers to the social reality that Mongolians encounter. And "it is this transnational pan-Mongolian solidarity between Mongols who live in China and Mongols who live across the border in Mongolia" that prompted the Chinese government to ban Teng Ge'er from performing on Chinese television (ibid.). Obviously, because of its content and symbolism, minority pop can raise sensitive issues. How this genre evolves will depend on the extent to which the government allows minorities to speak in their own voices.

This chapter has described the interface between Chinese and Euro-American music that has impacted music in both areas in significant ways. Multiple forces were at work beginning with the missionaries and other visitors to China. Other forces include Chinese musicians studying abroad, European musicians living and teaching in China, and the Chinese diaspora. Within China the music industry began to produce instruments, recordings, new listening habits, and music that aided in the construction of national music. Currently, Chinese music has a positive image and strong presence in the West. Its image has transformed from being considered noise to being appreciated by an international audience.

As for the impact of Western music in China, the adoption of Western music by Chinese musicians has forever changed the nature and foundation of Chinese music and practice. Western influence is not limited to just classical and academic music but has greatly affected popular music and popular culture as well. New styles of Chinese music are continually emerging as Chinese composers, inspired by Western music ideals, continue to refine their compositional techniques in creating new music. The fruitful exchange between Chinese and various types of Western music has resulted in a new synergy that benefits both and allows musicians to transcend the boundaries that once divided them.

CHAPTER 5

Music and Ideology

"If you are not a mandated ruler, you cannot regulate ritual and you cannot perform music."
Doctrine of the Mean, *chapter 28*

"If a man lacks benevolence, what has he to do with the rites? If a man lacks benevolence, what has he to do with music?"
Lunyu (*also known as the* Analects)

"To be a complete man, one has to rely on music."
Lunyu, *chapter 4*

In the previous chapters, I have discussed various kinds of music that have developed among commoners for entertainment, for self-expression, and to accompany festivities. Genres such as *jiangnan sizhu*, Cantonese opera, and *jingju* are representatives. As the quotes that open this chapter suggest, however, there are some genres of Chinese music that, more than music to please the ears, are closely related to specific philosophical and political viewpoints. The function of this music is to impress certain values upon listeners. Why is some music thought to be so powerful, and how does it work in the Chinese cultural context? In this chapter, I will explore the third theme of the book: music and ideology. I will discuss music for which the primary function is didactic or educational in nature and that is used in promoting a particular way of thinking.

CONFUCIANISM AND MUSIC
THROUGH TIME

In China, one of the earliest discussions of music and education can be found during the so-called Spring and Autumn periods (770–476 B.C.E.),

117

approximately twenty-five hundred years ago. A scholar philosopher called Kong zi, surname Kong (551–479 B.C.E.) and known in English as Confucius, developed a school of social thought—known as Confucianism—that has exerted a significant impact on the theory and practice of Chinese music for centuries since its inception.

Confucius developed a humanistic and functional approach to music, a view that considered music as a means of governance and self-cultivation. He denounced the use of music as entertainment, reasoning that music was a manifestation of virtue inherent in the universe itself. Because of its cosmological and numerological significance, it is one of the foundations of a properly ordered society. Therefore, he asserted that music and ritual would be an indispensable part of imperial court ceremony. He further established the paradigms of "proper music" (*yayue*) and "vernacular music" (*suyue*). According to Confucius, proper music promotes social harmony and vernacular music; that is, music that he considered sentimental and immoral leads to degeneration of one's mind and of society.

ACTIVITY 5.1 *The debate of how music influences society was not only shared by many ancient philosophers but can also be found in our own society. In 1985, Tipper Gore, wife of then Senator Al Gore, went before Congress to urge that labels be placed on records with explicit lyrics that are marketed to children. Investigate commentaries on the value and social influence of one genre, such as jazz, rock'n roll, rap, or hip-hop. In a short essay, compare and contrast how objections to these musics are different from or similar to the Confucian notion of proper versus bad music.*

To understand Confucian views on how music affects society, it is important to grasp the basic tenets of Confucianism. Confucius held that society was made up of five relationships: the relationships between husband and wife, parent and child, elder and younger sibling, elders and youngsters, and ruler and subject. This set of relationships is hierarchical and within it everyone is expected to observe specific roles and responsibilities. According to Confucian precepts, it is everyone's responsibility to regulate these relationships by behaving according to the mode of behavior described for each. When everyone fulfills his or her responsibilities, society will be in harmony. Following this line of reasoning based on familial relationships, a ruler has the important responsibility to ensure that the nation, as the highest order of family, is in order.

To ensure the maintenance of the five relationships, Confucius advocated the concepts of *ren* and *li*. The closest equivalent of *ren* is social virtue. He asserted that the virtues that help to maintain social harmony are benevolence, charity, sincerity, respectfulness, diligence, kindness, and goodness. *Li*, or social propriety, is the greatest principle of living. In his view, when society lives by *li*, it moves smoothly. Music is inseparable from *li* because proper music symbolizes the harmony between heaven and earth.

Proper music can also regulate one's mind and induce proper behavior. *Yayue* is the music of choice for the both the nation and the individual. A leader or ruler should ensure that proper music is performed in the court, while an individual should avoid music that corrupts the mind. Practicing proper music is the way to good behavior, and when all the relationships are properly maintained, society will become harmonious. Music can induce proper behavior so that the relationship between heaven and earth and between human behavior and morality are in order.

In a broad sense, ritual music included the state sacrificial ritual music, ancestral shrine ritual music, and Confucian ceremonial ritual music that were developed to honor Confucius after his death. Several types of music, such as songs, percussion music, and instrumental and vocal music, were performed in the rituals. Beginning in the Zhou dynasty (1027–221 B.C.E.), large orchestras made up of sets of bells, sets of stone chimes, drum, *guqin* (Figure 2.4), the long plucked zither *se*, *dizi* (Figure 1.9), *sheng* (Figure 1.11), and *xiao* (Figure 1.10) were to be used during these ceremonies. The songs were usually sung in slow and even tempo with four to eight beats per phrase corresponding to the number of words in the text. This music was stately and dignified with very little rhythmic variety. CD track 45 is a recording of a Confucian ceremony as it survived into the 1920s.

ACTIVITY 5.2 *Listen for the phrases of the music on CD track 45. Follow the initial three beats played first by drums and the fourth by the chimes that roughly established the tempo. Then pay attention to the length of the sustaining notes and the duration of the phrase. Describe the relationship between the accompaniment and the vocal part. How do you describe the*

singing style, texture, and tempo? Do they bear any resemblance to any of the regional music in chapter 3? In a short essay, summarize what you hear.

After the Zhou dynasty, ritual performance was regulated according to the context, time, and place. There were two types of music employed in every ritual. One was played by an ensemble performing in the main hall and the other by an ensemble in the courtyard. The indoor ensemble used a combination of melodic instruments and singing. The outdoor ensemble consisted only of instrumental music that was used to accompany dance by an even number of dancers arranged in rows performed during the rituals (Figure 5.1).

Depending on the rank and social status of the patron, the number of participants in the ritual varied. An emperor could have the largest number of musicians and dancers, a minister a slightly smaller group, and a lesser officer an even smaller group. In addition to vocal and instrumental music, for example, for a ritual in the imperial courts, an emperor could have sixty-four dancers, while a minister's ritual could only allow thirty-six dancers. Stylized movements formed an integral part of the ritual.

Although ritual ceremonial music had disappeared in China, it has been recently revived. Ritual ensembles in China have been promoted in Confucius' hometown of Qufu in Shandong province (Figure 1.2). In Korea, the court music genre known as *aak* has retained many features of ancient ancestral shrines and Confucian rituals. Confucian ritual has experienced a revival in Taiwan since the late 1960s and in China since the 1990s. The global interest in Confucian values has also fostered renewed interest in the relevance of Confucianism to contemporary living.

The Seven-Stringed Zither **Guqin.** *Guqin* or *qin* (Figure 5.2, CD track 37) is a seven-stringed plucked zither dating from ancient China. An instrument of cultural importance, *guqin* had a prominent role in court music and as a solo instrument played by scholars. Its association with royalty and scholars also meant that valuable information concerning its history, theory, practice, and aesthetics was recorded meticulously in writing.

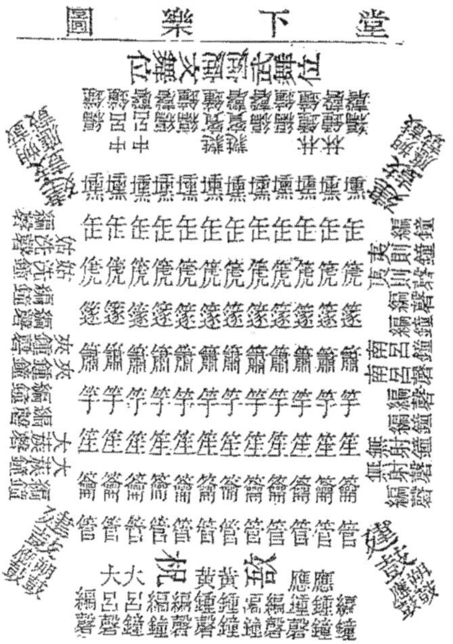

FIGURE 5.1 *Historical diagram of the setup for the instrumental ensemble in the courtyard. The four corners are occupied by drums of different sizes; wind instruments are in the center surrounded by bronze bells and stone chimes at four sides. The dancers are situated at the top of the diagram.* (Courtesy of Frederick Lau)

To understand the *guqin*'s long and complicated history, the famous Chinese musicologist Yang Yinliu (1899–1984) divided its history into three periods. The first period, from antiquity to 221 C.E., was dominated by stories about the mythical origin of the instrument. Arcahaeological discoveries of the *guqin* dated from the Shang dynasty confirmed that the instrument had existed as early as the fifteenth century B.C.E., making it one of the oldest instruments in China. It is believed that the *qin* became popular during this period as part of the court orchestra and as a solo instrument of the elite class.

The second period dates from around 221 B.C.E. in the Qin dynasty (221–207 B.C.E), to 907 C.E. in the Tang dynasty (618–907 C.E.). During this

FIGURE 5.2 *Scholar playing the* guqin.
(Courtesy of Frederick Lau)

period, guqin music was influenced by Confucian ideology, the Daoist philosophy of noninterference and simplicity, and Central Asian music that was imported into the court and entertainment music of the Sui (581–618) and Tang (618–907) dynasties. It is also during this period that attempts were made to codify guqin playing techniques and music notation. "You Lan" ("Elegant Orchid," Figure 5.4), which has been dated to the sixth century, is known as the the the first notated piece of guqin music. From that time, playing *guqin* music became increasingly popular among the literati. In the third period, from the tenth century to the twentieth century, a proliferation of *guqin* compositions and refinement of playing techniques emerged. During the Sung dynasty (960–1279), hundreds of poems and essays on the *qin* were created by the literati. Considered the golden period of *guqin* music, many well-known pieces can be dated from this period. As a convention of literati culture, its music and playing techniques were documented in treatises and handbooks (Figure 5.3). It is during this period that aesthetic considerations became the most important aspect of *guqin* playing.

This history of *guqin* shows that the instrument was established as an elite instrument and was played by elites. *Guqin* has long been venerated for its mythical and cultural importance. Confucius is believed to have been an active player of the *guqin*. It was once recorded that the sound of the *guqin* was so mesmerizing that it caused Confucius

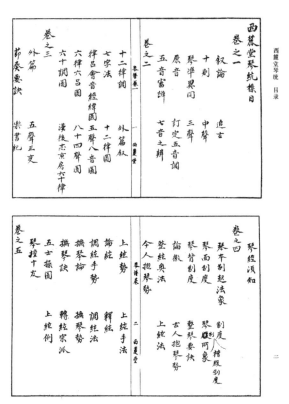

FIGURE 5.3 *Inside page of a* guqin *handbook. (Courtesy of Frederick Lau)*

to ignore even the good taste of meat. This is an example illustrating Confucius' high regard for the instrument and its power and symbolism. It was generally believed that the proper playing of the *guqin* could lead one to spiritual enlightenment. According to Confucianism, purity of mind is one of the accomplishments of a complete person and cultivating and rectifying one's mind can lead to this state. Thus the *guqin* became a symbol of literary life and playing the *guqin* was seen as a purifying sort of meditation. Playing the *guqin* became an act of self-purification that could lead one to spiritual enlightenment and, by extension, a harmonious world. In other words, playing the *guqin* is a symbolic manifestation of the Confucian philosophy of self, society, and cosmology. During the Han period (202 B.C.E.–220 C.E.), the concept that the *guqin* was the unique symbol of all correct and accomplished music was consolidated.

The music of the *guqin* was well documented in many treatises and handbooks. These written sources usually appear in the form of an anthology containing valuable information about the music and its practice. These handbooks provide not only detailed descriptions of playing techniques, history of the *guqin,* and its connection to literary sources but also notation of *qin* music as transmitted by a master or within a school of *guqin* playing.

The music notation is of particular interest because it is different from the traditional *gongche* notation (Figure 2.6), which shows pitches and rhythm. The earliest form of notation is written in a prose form known as *wenzipu* (Figure 5.4). The descriptions give detailed instruction to the player about where to place the fingers and the manner of striking the strings. This form of prose was later simplified to an abbreviated character notation known as *jianzipu* (Figure 5.5). In this notation, parts of the normal Chinese characters are extracted to form new codes. Each code represents one specific finger action (Figure 5.6), and a series of codes are combined together to indicate a continuous motion for both hands (Figure 5.7). Left and right hands are indicated by the placement of the code in the composite block. Players have to learn to read the codes before putting them into action.

The process of realizing the notation in practice is known as *dapu.* During this process, the player would first decipher each symbol in the text (Yung 1985). Since the notation only provides the manner of striking the strings and where to place the lefthand fingers, the player has to determine the length of each note or series of notes according to the style and performance practice of his lineage. This is also where individual creativity comes into play. *Dapu* requires more than technical knowledge of how to realize the symbols and codes in performance; a player should also be well versed in literature and history in order to interpret properly the extra meaning of the music.

Guqin music, like almost all Chinese music, is programmatic in nature. The music depicts a scene in nature or narrates a story. Titles such as "Geese Landing on a Sandy Beach," "Moon over the Border Gate and Mountain," "The Variations on the Plum Blossoms Theme," and "Flowing Water" are excellent examples of programmatic titles that are poetic and contemplative in tone. Understanding meaning implied in the titles would allow the player to identify the mood of the composition and the intent of the music.

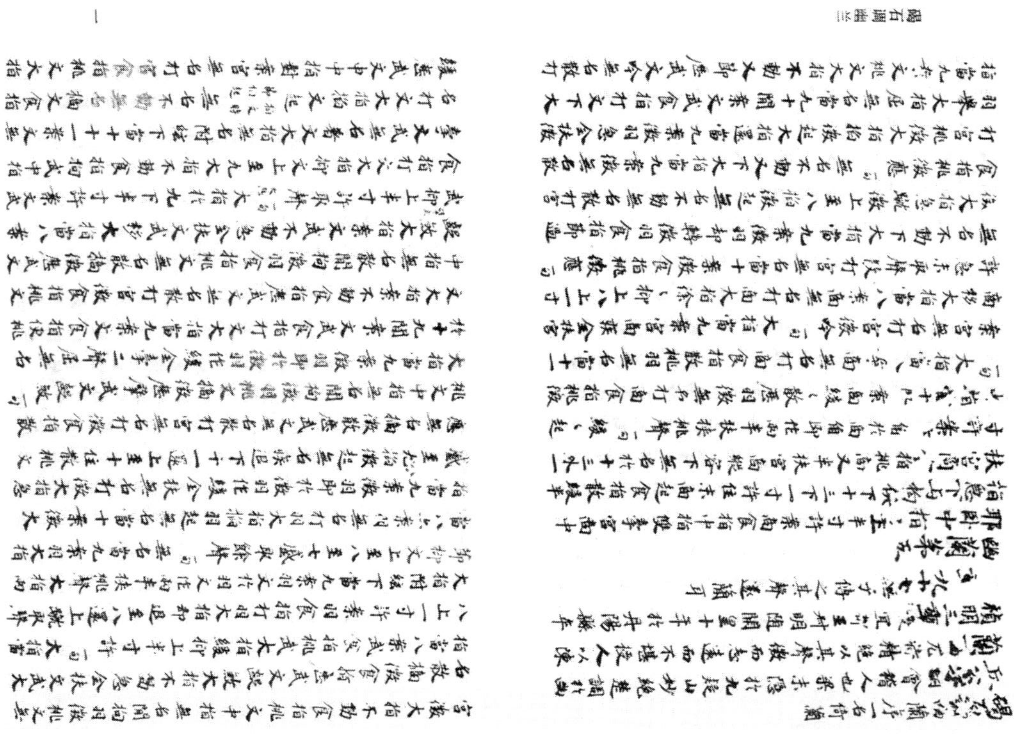
碣石調幽蘭　一
碣石調幽蘭序一名倚蘭
丘公字明會稽人也梁末隱於九疑山妙絕楚調於幽
蘭一曲尤特精絕以其聲微而志遠而不堪授人以陳
禎明三年授宜都王叔明隨開皇十年於丹陽縣卒
年九十七無子傳之其聲遂簡耳
幽蘭第五
耶臥中指十上半寸許案商食指中指雙牽宮商中
指急下與構俱下十三下一寸許住末商起食指散緩半
扶宮商食指挑商又半扶宮商縱容下無名於十三外一
寸許案々角於商角即作兩半扶挑聲　一句　緩々起
上指食十上案商緩々散歷羽徵無名打商食指挑徵
一句　大指當八無名當無名打商食指散挑羽無名當十一
案宮無名打宮徵吟　一句　大指當九案宮商疾全扶宮
商移大指當八案商無名打商大指徐々抑上八上一寸
許急未取聲設打宮無名當十案徵食指挑徵應　一句
無名不動下大指當九案徵羽却轉徵羽食指節過
徵大指急蹴徵上至八指徵起無名不動無名散打宮
食指挑徵應　一句　無名不動又下大指當九案徵無名散
打宮挑徵大指掐徵起大指還當九案徵羽急全扶徵
羽舉大指屈無名當九十間案文武食指打文下大
指當九案々文挑文大指不動又節歷武文吟無名散打
宮徵大指不動食指挑文中指無名間拘羽徵挑文無
名散摘徵食指歷武文起斂大指不動急全扶文武大
指當八案武食指挑武大指緩抑上半寸許　一句　大指當
八上一寸許案羽食指打羽大指却退至八還上蹴取聲
大指附絃下當九案羽文於羽文作兩半扶挑聲大指兩
節抑文上至八至七盛取餘聲　一句　無名當九案羽大指
當八上案羽無名打羽大指掏羽起無名當十案徵大
指當九案徵羽即於徵羽作緩全扶無名打徵大指急
蹴至七指徵起無名疾退下十一還上至十住散挑文
應無名摘徵散歷武文無名散打宮無名打徵食指散
挑文中指無名間拘徵羽挑文摘徵歷摩武文起斂　一句
大指當九案徵羽即於徵羽作緩全牽二聲屈無名
於十九間案文武食指打文大指當九案文食指便挑
文大指案不動食指歷武文無名散打宮徵食指挑文
中指無名散間拘徵羽食指挑文無名散摘徵應武文
起斂大指案文武不動急全扶文武移大指當八案
武抑上半寸許取聲　一句　引上　大指於九下半寸許案文武
食指打文大指抑文上至九大指不動食指拘武中指
牽文武無名著文大指無名附絃下當十十一案文無
名打文大指掐文起　掐文時如何起　無名不動無名摘文食指
緩應武文中中指對案宮無名打宮食指挑文大指

FIGURE 5.4　Guqin wenzipu. *The text reads from right to left, top to bottom.* (Courtesy of Frederick Lau)

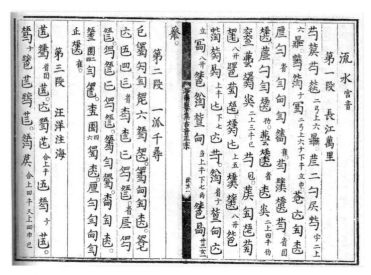

FIGURE 5.5 Guqin Jianzipu *abbreviated character notation. As in Chinese writings, the music and text are written from right to left and top to bottom. The title of the piece appears on the far right, followed by the mode of the piece. A short poetic description of the piece sometimes will be included in the next line. This is the opening page to the piece "Liushui" (CD track 37).* (Courtesy of Frederick Lau)

Most *guqin* pieces are sectional (CD track 37). They start with an introduction and move through different sections that can be identified as *rudiao* (establish meter), *ruman* (slow down), and *weisheng* (conclusion). The progression is from slow to fast and gradually slows again. The music usually starts and concludes with several measures of short harmonics.

Because it is an instrument built for an individual, the volume of the *guqin* is soft. When listening to *guqin* music, one has to pay close attention to the subtle change of tone color. The music contains many glissandi of pitches, different ways of striking the strings, and subtle manipulations of color. The goal of the music is not to excite one's senses but to use the *guqin* as a tool that leads to spiritual contemplation. This is why the *guqin* emerges as a symbol for the elite and scholarly classes, people who have access to the privilege of leisurely pursuits.

Stud Positions

1	2	3	4	5	6	7	8	9	10	11	12	13
一	二	三	四	五	六	七	八	九	十	十一	十二	十三

Left Hand Symbols

大　Thumb

中　Middle finger

夕　Ring finger

イ　Index finger

Right Hand Symbols

勹　Middle finger pulls a string

尸　Thumb pulls a string with nail

早　Pluck 2 strings simultaneously

丁　Ring finger plucks a string inward

凵　Index finger plucks a string outward

FIGURE 5.6   *Lefthand notation (left) and righthand notation (right).*

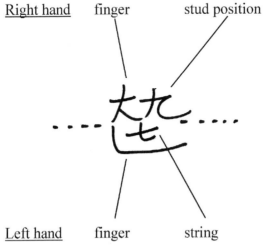

FIGURE 5.7   *Composite block showing a continuous motion with both hands.*

ACTIVITY 5.3 *Listen to the* guqin *piece "Liushui" ("Flowing Water," CD track 37). "Liushui" first appeared in the famous fifteenth-century collection* Shen Qi Mi Pu (The Handbook of Spiritual and Marvelous Mysteries), *one of the earliest large collections of* guqin *music. Before the Tang dynasty, Liushui was a piece that contained two distinct sections entitled "High Mountain" and "Flowing Water." These two parts later became two independent pieces. The version heard in this recording was recorded by the famous modern* qin *player Guan Ping Hu (1891–1967) in the 1960s. Guan, an influential player who promoted* guqin *music, was famous for his performance and rendition of "Liushui." This version is performed according to his own* dapu, *a process of realizing the abbreviated notation in sound.*

There are nine sections in Guan Ping Hu's rendition of "Liushui" on CD track 37. The following table shows the timing of the sections. The musical characteristics of each section are highlighted for reference. This piece is considered to be technically challenging because of the different kinds of finger techniques it calls for.

Time	Section	Characteristics
0:00–0:37	Introduction	Slow and stately (*ruidiao*)
0:38–1:18	II	Dominated by harmonics
1:19–1:41	III	Harmonics, played at an octave higher than section II
1:42–2:20	IV (*ruman*)	Slightly faster, main melody
2:21–2:51	V	Development of material in section IV
2:52–3:38	VI	Lots of fast long and short glissandi, imitating the sound of flowing streams
3:39–4:56	VII	Slower tempo and harmonics in higher register
4:57–5:19	VIII	Faster tempo and Louder, using material in section IV
6:19–6:36		Series of short glissando as in the second part of section VI
6:37–7:12	IX (*weisheng*)	Similar to the introduction, with an octave jump
7:13–7:36	Conclusion	Short passage dominated by harmonics

Because the *qin* has been linked closely to the literati, its practice, musical aesthetic, and symbolism have been shaped largely by the values of the literati. Understanding *qin* music and its history therefore cannot be separated from Confucian theories of society, virtue, human relationships, and cosmological relationships.

Amateur Music Clubs.   As discussed in chapter 1, the Confucian ideal was not only confined to ritual music but also affected music of commoners and the literati. According to Confucius, education of the individual is a necessary step in becoming an "exemplary person" (*junzi*), one who is compassionate and virtuous and who has supreme ethical and moral stances. Given the prominence of music as one of the arts for educating a superior person, it is easy to understand why amateur music-making has played such an important role in the life of scholars, including commoners. In addition to studying the classical texts, a scholar should also practice the "six arts." These six arts, together with the studying of classical Great Books, complete the steps necessary for one to become a *junzi,* "superior person." They include ritual, music, archery, riding, calligraphy, and mathematics.

Based on this thinking, practicing music as self-cultivation rather than to make a living was in line with Confucian thought. To this end, there were several amateur ensemble traditions whose practitioners considered their practices to be Confucian music, *ruyue.* Although this genre of music has little to do with the music of the Confucian ritual, the act of participating in music-making as amateurs exemplified the participants' Confucian notion of self-cultivation and personal improvement.

There are several regional genres considered part of the *ruyue* family. The *nanguan* of Fujian province (CD track 30), the *xianshi* of Chaozhou area (CD track 13), and the "music of the *Han,*" *hanyue,* of the Hakka people are all indirectly linked to the Confucian ideal of cultivating a superior person (Figure 5.8). What these ensemble traditions have in common is that they were all performed by amateurs and mostly by men for their own enjoyment. It is their goals and intentions that distinguished players in these ensembles from other professional musicians.

In urban areas during the nineteenth century, the practice of amateur music-making in music clubs began to gain popularity among the literate upper classes in urban areas. In music clubs, the cultivation of the mind, the act of participating, and the elevation of the sentiments were elevated above musical skills. Amateur music clubs emerged whose names contained words like *ya* (elegant), *qing* (pure), *ru* (Confucian), *datong*

FIGURE 5.8 Handiao/*Chaozhou* xianshi *performance. This ensemble plays both* handiao *and Chaozhou* xianshi; *the instrumentation is similar, except the* erxian *is the leading instrument in* xianshi. *From left:* yangqin, *percussion (in back)* tixian, pipa, *and* sanxian. *(Courtesy of Frederick Lau)*

(big harmony), and *yi* (leisure), words that embody a heavy sense of Confucian sentiment. Participating in amateur musical activities not only fulfilled an esthetic and pleasurable social function but also tacitly marked a person's taste, class, and social status because amateur pursuit of arts and music was a highly revered virtue for the literati in the Confucian worldview. This practice continues today in many Chinese-speaking communities outside China. Although on the surface these music clubs appeared to be a kind of gentlemen's club, their existence owed much to Confucian ideals.

DONGJING MUSIC OF THE *NAXI* PEOPLE

Confucianism not only was popular among the Han majority but was also adopted by some non-Han ethnic groups as a symbolic means to define their elite and urban status against those who were considered less "civilized" and "educated" because they continued to adhere to the indigenous way of thinking. The case of the *Naxi dongjing* music is a good example of how the adoption of Confucianist practices created a new way of redefining social class and identity.

The *Naxi* is a minority group living in the *Naxi* Autonomous County of Lijing in the Yunnan province in southwestern China (Figure 1.2). The *Naxi* ethnic group has its own language and belief system that is a form of indigenous shamanism called *dongba*. Because of cultural interaction between the *Han* and *Naxi* people, the *Naxi* upper class has absorbed many Han practices as markers of sophistication and elite social status. Helen Rees, one of the leading experts on *Naxi* music, reports that by the late nineteenth century Han operatic forms were frequently performed in Lijiang by traveling performing troupes. Local *Naxi* groups also began to perform local provincial opera in the *Han* language. The various activities showed that Han culture was firmly established among the *Naxi*.

As early as the beginning of the nineteenth century, associations for a Han-influenced music called *dongjing* were popular in urban and affluent areas of the region. These "amateur musical-ritual" societies often performed elaborate ritual music that included chanting, singing, and playing of *Han* instruments such as *erhu, pipa,* and *dizi* (CD track 46). Members of these associations were local male literati who could read and write Chinese. Their knowledge of elite *Han* culture explains why their scores are written in Chinese characters and the music is written in the *Han* notation.

In *dongjing* music, the *Naxi* adopted a practice that is similar to the silk and bamboo music I discussed in chapter 1. All the instrumentalists perform the basic melodic line and each offers a slightly varied rendition of the melody, thus producing a heterophonic texture. Scholars consider these musical features striking hallmarks of *Han* music. When adopted by the *Naxi* people, these features added another layer of meaning to *dongjing* music because they also signified the local elite's status by displaying its knowledge of *Han* music and Confucianist ideals.

Of all the *Han*-influenced music, the most widely known genre among the *Naxi* people since the 1970s is *dongjing* music, called *Naxi guyue* ("*Naxi* ancient music"). Since the 1990s, tourism to Lijiang has increased dramatically. A visit to the local *dongjing* association is almost a must for any visitor who wants to experience one of the oldest musics in the region.

MUSIC AND IDEOLOGY IN THE PRC

In the world today all culture, all literature and art belong to definite classes and are geared to definite political lines. There is in fact no such thing as art for art's sake, art that stands above classes, art that is detached from or independent of politics. Proletarian literature and

> *art are part of the whole proletarian revolutionary cause; they use,*
> *as Lenin said, cogs and wheels in the whole revolutionary machine.*
>
> From Mao Zedong, Talks at the Yenan Forum on Literature
> and Art, 1942, Selected Works, Vol. III

As the previous section illustrated, music has played an important role in the dissemination of social values and for educational purposes since the time of Confucius. Although his notions of *yayue* ("elegant music") and *suyue* ("secular music") may no longer be directly relevant in the modern era, the notion that music can affect people's behavior and thinking continues to work in Chinese society.

The 1949 Chinese Communist Revolution marked a significant turning point in the history of modern China. The Chinese Communist Party (CCP), led by Mao Zedong, defeated the Chiang Kai Shek–led Chinese Republic Party Kuomingtang (KMT) and established its political dominance in China, forcing the KMT government to leave China for Taiwan. In post-1949 China, one of the primary political goals for the communist government has been the construction of a socialist society and new national image to distinguish itself from the social and political system of the defeated KMT government (1911–1949). The framework for this socialist transformation is based entirely on the Marxist-Leninist political doctrine and Mao Zedong's thought.

To establish a new society and identity, the CCP government carried out massive reforms in all domains of society. Crucial to the establishment of images of national unity in socialist China was the use of emblematic cultural forms intended to articulate and maintain links between the party and the masses. Projects promoting traditional cultural forms and styles that had been associated with the "common people" were strongly supported and encouraged (chapter 2). At the same time, the government also supported new compositions and genres based on styles that it approved as propaganda. Among various forms of cultural and social expressions, music was determined to be one of the essential resources for the state in the creation of ideological ground. Once new styles in music, literature, painting, and dance were defined and materialized in practice, they clearly functioned as emblems for the state in representing itself in the popular perception.

The state ideology, inserted into all social and cultural practices, hence became the dominant worldview through which the public had to redefine its perception and aesthetics. Anyone who resisted or challenged this dominant official view was subjected to ideological rectification, reeducation camps, or suppression, such as the Hundred

Flower Movement in 1964, the 1957 Anti-Rightist Campaign, and the Tiananmen massacre of June 1989. The Chinese state, which has taken an active role in providing political and cultural leadership, presents itself as the voice of the people. To enforce this, various forms of musical production, which symbolize and are embedded in the state populist ideology, are specifically defined and promoted by the state. State ideology has subsequently been adopted and echoed by musicians and music writers alike across the country; this is demonstrated clearly in writings that emphasize the integration of music with revolutionary elements and "correct" ideology. Music and other forms of cultural production are supervised closely and monitored under the control of the central government. The following section explores three different types of music that emerged beginning in 1949. Although they vary in practice and sound, they share the goal of disseminating political messages.

Revolutionary Songs for the Masses.   Revolutionary songs, *geming gequ,* or mass songs, *qunzhong gequ,* are songs that contain explicit political messages written for the glorification and support of the CCP. Different from Chinese vocal folk songs or narratives that are appreciated for their entertainment value, mass songs are designed to arouse audiences' emotions and to motivate people to support government policies. Simply put, mass songs are a type of music whose sole purpose is to transmit specific political messages and ideology. What makes them unique is that the lyrics contain explicit references to politics. This kind of song became popularized in the early twentieth century after the establishment of the CCP in 1922.

Mass songs were either written in the Western song style with a simple melody and chordal accompaniment or inspired by Chinese folk tunes. In strophic form, each stanza contains new lyrics while the melody remains the same. The music is marchlike in character, often upbeat and in a major key to impart good spirit. The melody is usually easy to remember because these songs are designed to be sung in unison in public political gatherings and rallies. Because these new compositions are usually short, simple, and easy to learn, they became a powerful tool through which the party could communicate with the general public.

The content of mass songs covers a wide range of topics that are related to the political ideology and achievements of the CCP. They can be categorized into groups according to themes and content. The themes include songs that glorify Chairman Mao, praise the CCP, commemorate regions associated with the revolution, promote political campaigns, recount class struggles, express people's gratitude toward the party, promote national unity among the national minorities, and praise the work of workers, peasants, and soldiers. I include here translations of two of the most famous mass songs, "East Is Red" ("Dongfang Hong," CD track 47) and "I Love Beijing's Tiananmen" ("Wo ai Beijing de Tiananmen," CD track 48). The lyrics of "Dongfang Hong" were attributed to a northern Shaanxi province farmer, Li Youyuan, who set them to melody from a local folk song from the region. It is believed that Li got his inspiration upon seeing the rising sun in the morning of a sunny day and associated it with the glory of Chairman Mao.

"East Is Red"	"Dongfang Hong"
The east is red, the sun rises	Dongfanghong, taiyangsheng
China has brought forth a Mao Zedong	Dongfang chuliaoge Mao Zedong
He brings fortune to the people	Ta wei remin mou xingfu
Hu er hei yo, he is the savior for the people	Hu'er heiyo, tashi renmin da jiuxing
Chairman Mao loves the people	Maozhuxi ai remin
He is our guide	Ta shi women de dai lu ren
To build a new China	Weiliao jianshe xin Zhongguo
Hu er hei yo, he leads us forward	Hu'er heiyo, lingdao women xiang qianjin
The Communist Party is like the sun	Gongchangdang xiang taiyang
Wherever it shines, there is light	Zhaodao nail nail liang
Wherever there is a Communist Party	Nali you liao gonchangdang
Hu er hei yo, there the people are free	Hu'er hei yo,nail renmin jiefang

"Dongfang Hong" was perhaps one of the most famous songs during the Cultural Revolution in the 1960s. Because it was heard so frequently, it was considered the de facto anthem of the PRC. During the Cultural Revolution (1966–1976), the song was played through loudspeaker systems in every city and village across the country. The people at every work unit were expected to sing the song in unison every morning, and students sang it in schools before the first class of the day. Political rallies, public gatherings, and broadcast programs usually began with this song. The political message in this song is clear, and singing the song is a show of respect affirming the greatness of the party. The text repeats the image of Chairman Mao as the great leader. The simple text shows dedication to Chairman Mao and the nation's policies under his leadership. It also reiterates the importance of the Beijing and Tiananmen. Beijing is the capital and the administrative central of the nation. Tiananmen is a huge square in the center of Beijing strategically placed adorning the Forbidden Palace of Imperial China, and it is the place where Mao stood high to greet crowds. A portray of Mao is hung on top of the fortlike gate that overlooks the square.

"I Love Beijing's Tiananmen"	"Wo ai Beijing de Tian'anmen"
I love Beijing's Tiananmen, the sun rises over Tiananmen	Wo ai Beijing Tian'anmen, Tian'anmen shang taiyang-sheng
Our great leader Chairman Mao, guides us forward.	Women weidai de Maozhuxi, zhiyin women xiang qianjin
I love Beijing's Tiananmen, the sun rises over Tiananmen	Wo ai Beijing Tian'anmen, Tian'anmen shang taiyang-sheng
Our great leader chairman Mao, guides us forward.	Women weidai de Maozhuxi xiang qianjin
I love Beijing's Tiananmen, the sun rises over Tiananmen	Wo ai Beijing Tian'anmen, Tian'anmen shang taiyang-sheng
Our great leader chairman Mao, guides us forward.	Women weidai de Maozhuxi xiang qianjin

ACTIVITY 5.4 *Look up Tiananmen Square on the Internet to see photos and articles that explain its significance in recent Chinese history. Take notes so that your findings can be added to those of others in a classroom discussion.*

Model Opera: **Yangbanxi.** The name *yangbanxi,* or "model opera," refers to a group of modern *jingju* that contain newly composed music and highly politicized plots. Emerging in the 1960s, *yangbanxi* was endorsed by the government and became the only music that was allowed to be performed during the Cultural Revolution (1967–1977). These operas' special status turned them into "models" for other operas throughout the country. Often seen as the brainchild of Mao's wife, Jiang Qing, model opera became the poster child of the government's policy of transforming traditional art forms into genres acceptable to the government.

From the start, *yangbanxi* was steeped in politics. When the government began to measure traditional operas against the newly instituted artistic standard of the post-1949 era, it concluded that traditional operas were harmful to the new society because they were seen as products of Chinese feudal society. Characters in traditional operas were mostly about important historical figures and people drawn from the upper class, such as emperors, generals, scholars, and nobility. Mao openly criticized traditional operas as feudalistic, class based, and superstitious and demanded that a new revolutionary opera be created based on the proletarian ideology. To purge traditional operas of their feudalistic association, traditional operas had to be rewritten and recalibrated. In addition, many new operas with revolutionary themes were subsequently created with new plots focusing on the common people that the party valued, such as workers, peasants, soldiers, and female revolutionaries (Figure 5.9).

FIGURE 5.9 *Poster of a scene from a "model opera"* (yangbanxi). *(Courtesy of Frederick Lau)*

ACTIVITY 5.5 *Compare Figure 5.9 with Figure 3.3. What are the most striking similarities and differences between the two?*

Beginning in the 1960s, Mao's wife Jiang Qing began to assert her influence and started to revise a number of *jingju* using contemporary themes and her own interpretation of the communist ideology. The first two works that she produced were *Hongdengji* (*Story of the Red Lantern*) and *Shajiabang* (*Shajia Village*). Jiang Qing continued with two more reformed operas, *Zhiqu weihushan* (*Taking the Tiger Mountain by Strategy*) and *Qixi baihutuan* (*Raid on the White Tiger Regiment*).

The stories in all the *yangbanxi* follow a similar plot about the struggle between communist soldiers and their aggressors and recount how the final victory was won. They were effective publicity tools for the CCP to disseminate its ideology and political messages. For example, the plot in *Shajiabang* is a telling example. This story takes place in the town of Shajiabang during the Anti-Japanese War era (1930s–1940s). The town came under attack by Japanese and Republican troops. Eventually the town was liberated by the arrival of the New People's Army and local underground grassroots fighters. Shajiabang was liberated by the New Fourth Army and became a center of guerrilla warfare against the Japanese. The party is portrayed as the benefactor of all oppressed people. The opera praises the courage and bravery of the New People's Army and the determination of the party to protect its people.

Jiang Qing's works were performed in 1964 for the first time at an Opera Festival in Shanghai. It was during that time that these reformed operas were officially called "model operas." *Yangbanxi* relies on essential musical elements from *jingju*, such as the use of the bowed lute *jinghu*, singing style, and percussion, but they are juxtaposed or at times combined with innovative ideas. For instance, instead of having a small traditional ensemble with *jinghu* as the leading accompaniment for the singing (as shown in chapter 2), a small orchestra of Western strings and woodwinds was included as part of the ensemble, adding a range of new sounds. Unlike traditional *jingju*, the role of the percussion was greatly diminished. The vocal quality and timbre were changed to the *bel canto* style (a song-singing style originating in Italy) in order to fit into the new musical and artistic constraints (CD track 49). Because *yangbanxi* is a product of a political movement, its music and plot therefore were highly eclectic in content and appearance.

ACTIVITY 5.4 *Listening to CD track 49 and compare it to the* jingju *excerpts on CD tracks 26 and 29, paying close attention to the voice quality and the use of accompaniment. How would you describe the tempo and texture of the music? Similarly, if you compare CD track 49 with CD track 40, what insight can you draw? Finally, from the four vocal excerpts mentioned here, what have you learned about Chinese singing styles?*

During the Cultural Revolution, *yangbanxi* was one of the few politically correct vocal genres endorsed and supported by the government; most European and traditional Chinese music were banned. *Yangbanxi,* alongside genres such as *zhandi xinge* ("new songs of the battlefield") and *yuluge* ("quotation songs"), was the "official" musical form permitted to be performed in public. Thus, many regional styles of *yangbanxi* were created. To ensure that the music was properly adopted and the meaning and political messages unchanged, published music scores and recordings of the famous operas were readily available. Many regional styles of *yangbanxi* were created.

Some of the more famous operatic music was rearranged for symphonic instruments and piano. Since the music is highly programmatic, it effectively conveys the same political messages to its audiences that the opera does. For instance, arias from the opera *The Red Lantern* were rewritten as a cantata accompanied by piano during that time. The story of *The Red Lantern* is about the determination of a young girl to follow the example of her father to carry on with the revolution. Even as an instrumental piece, the music is tied to the story. Similarly, the music of *Shajiabang* was transformed into a symphonic work for full orchestra, but the notion of patriotism derived from the original plot of defending the nation from the invading Japanese of the 1930s, could not escape those who saw the opera. Although Western instruments were banned during this period, they were allowed to be performed because the music was based on the model operas.

After the end of the Cultural Revolution, *yangbanxi* fell out of favor because of its association with the political turmoil of the Cultural Revolution. Despite its history, however, *yangbanxi* has made a big comeback in recent years. For those caught up in the fad of "Mao craze," the music of *yangbanxi* has become an icon of nostalgia and imagination that has lost its association with politics. The "Mao craze" is a fetishization and idolization of Mao that eventually led many people to start collecting Mao memorabilia and objects from the Cultural Revolution.

FIGURE 5.10 *CD cover from a recent release of* yangbanxi. *(Courtesy of Frederick Lau)*

Like Mao buttons, jackets, and Mao's Little Red Book, songs and CD sets of *yangbanxi* are available in karaoke bars and sung at parties and private gatherings (Figure 5.10). The recent popularity of *yangbanxi* songs also reminds the modern audience how powerful and politically important this genre once was. Ironically, *yangbanxi* is again caught in another kind of politics, that is, the politics of consumerism as China moves into a new global market economy where consumption of the past is a big business.

CONCLUSION

The case studies presented in this chapter demonstrate different ways that certain musical elements have been utilized strategically to inspire a particular way of thinking, whether the music is promoted by one person or under the guidance of the state. The development of new musical practice can, in effect, symbolize the privilege of class and authority, as in the case of *qin* music, and authority and ideology, as in the case of the new communist state's dominance and political ideology in mass songs or *yangbanxi*. For music and ideology to work hegemonically (Gramsci 1971), control over forms of cultural production and artistic discourse is required as well as acceptance by those who would be controlled. It is through this process that the advocates of the Confucian way of conceptualizing human relationships and the communist government shaped music to create and maintain systems of thought.

In achieving its political and ideological goals, the CCP is faced with the problem of dealing with traditions of the past that clash with the ideology of the present. To maintain control, new practices that manifest the dominant communist ideology have to be created to replace these older traditions. In Mao's own words, "We do not by any means refuse to use the old forms of the feudal and the bourgeois, but in our hands these old forms are reconstructed and filled with new content, so that they also become revolutionary and serve the people" (McDougall 1980: 65). By encouraging the creation of new art forms and incorporating new meaning into traditional forms, artistic productions in the post-1949 period underscore the formation of new traditions by processes of strategy and choice. The selection and manipulation of certain elements from traditional culture are powerful methods by which the state can advance its political goals.

All of these case studies support the point that music and its production can be manipulated for ideological ends and that under such conditions music and ideology are intertwined. The relationship between meaning on the one hand and musical practice on the other is fluid; consequently, music can be transformed to suit specific sociopolitical situations.

CHAPTER 6

Chinese Music beyond China

In this final chapter, I return once again to the theme of identity and music-making but this time from the perspective of Chinese who have been living outside China. In particular, I focus on the role of Chineseness in determining the genre and style of Chinese music that is appropriate to a social context. As I have explained in previous chapters, Chinese music is context specific rather than based on essentialized notions of Chinese sound. Three interrelated forces are at work in the process: memory, nostalgia, and imagination. Each of these forces dictates a choice of music and style of performance. My interest in overseas Chinese music began after I walked past a Chinese music club in San Francisco's Chinatown. Drawn by the sound of the instruments coming from an upstairs apartment, I was curious to know why these overseas Chinese continued to play Chinese music in their adopted country and whether such music-making is an isolated phenomenon. My curiosity led me on a journey during which I encountered a world of Chinese music-making connected to yet different from what I experienced in China.

While some forms of music found in Chinese communities abroad may sound similar to musical practices in China, others have transformed into what may be described as fusion or hybridized music. Unlike the sense of identity held by those who never left the country, notions of "Chineseness" for overseas Chinese musicians have been shaped by the social conditions and cultural diversity of their host countries. These external factors directly affect musical practices and stretch the term *Chinese music*. The boundaries of Chinese music are further extended with the rising popularity of Chinese music in the contemporary global music scene. Beyond styles, the function and meaning of the music have also been transformed in new contexts. The information provided in this chapter is centered around two major questions: How do overseas Chinese experiences affect the production and image of Chinese music? How has "Chineseness" been expressed musically in global contexts?

EXPRESSING CHINESENESS MUSICALLY

Migration of Chinese to other parts of the world started before the thirteenth century. Beginning in the nineteenth century, large numbers of Chinese from southern China began to migrate overseas in search of jobs and fortune. The emergence of maritime trade brought many Chinese coastal dwellers to Southeast Asia and beyond. The mid-nineteenth century Gold Rush brought a large wave of workers from Canton province to the West Coast of America and Australia. Most of these Chinese migrants were sojourners—that is, they intended to return home after they made enough money—but many ended up settling down in their adopted countries.

As migrants and minorities in the new countries, these sojourners relied on memories of their home culture to define a sense of self and cultural grounding for the new environment. Their experiences, based either on nostalgia for or memory of homeland culture, inevitably informed the music they practiced. There is little question in their minds that what they chose to play is "Chinese music," albeit redefined by their context. However, the situation is different for their offspring who were born and raised outside China. For them, Chineseness is often "imagined" or "constructed" out of a knowledge of Chinese culture and music that has been filtered through multiple cultural lenses and processes. Given these cultural and generational differences, it is easy to see why Chinese music in the diaspora is multifaceted rather than a monolithic category. The diversity of Chinese music outside China reflects the creative ways that different Chinese communities and individuals have interpreted and internalized Chineseness. Diasporic Chinese music-making ranges from music that recalls various traditional genres of music discussed in previous chapters to some innovative forms that only make passing reference to traditional sound and elements. Regardless of the end product, traditional music has been a vital source of inspiration for overseas musicians.

TRADITIONAL MUSIC IN THE DIASPORA

Amateur Chinese music clubs have been popular in overseas Chinese communities since the mid-nineteenth century, but these clubs differ in terms of practice and organization. Initially established to provide entertainment for new immigrants, these voluntary social groups perform music that evoked memories of the homeland. As essential agents in maintaining a sense of Chinese regional identity, these clubs invariably became keepers of Chinese culture and were a source of cultural capital from which participants could draw. These multiple functions of music clubs are prevalent in many overseas communities. The following example provides a detailed account of how a club works in one specific locale.

Cantonese Music Clubs in the New World. Cantonese opera was developed in the mid-nineteenth century and quickly became a popular genre among urbanites and commoners in Guangdong province. According to studies of Cantonese opera in the United States, Cantonese opera has long been popular in cities such as San Francisco, New York, and Honolulu (Riddle 1983; Chan 1997). In these cities, apart from hosting visiting troupes, local Cantonese opera clubs became centers of community life. For instance, there are currently four Cantonese opera clubs in Honolulu, at least eight Cantonese music clubs were active in New York Chinatown in the 1990s (Chan 1997: 326), and numerous large and small ones operate in the San Francisco Bay area. Similar to the functions of the music clubs I described earlier, most Cantonese opera clubs were established to provide entertainment and venues for social interaction.

The migration of a large number of Cantonese to North America promoted the popularity of Cantonese music in the region. Cantonese opera has been performed from coast to coast by local and traveling groups, making it one of the most well-known genres of Chinese music in the United States. Because of the migration of Cantonese to other parts of the world, Cantonese music clubs are also popular wherever there is a sizable Cantonese community.

Cantonese opera troupes were known in the West as early as the nineteenth century. As described earlier, a U.S. concert presenter contracted a famous Cantonese opera troupe, Tong Hook Tong, to perform in New York City and San Francisco in mid-nineteenth century (Tchen 1999: 86). Unfortunately, due to mishandling of funds and bad management, the troupe had to be disbanded in New York City. Later, professional Cantonese opera troupes traveled to the United States, because the demand for Cantonese opera performances corresponded to the rising Cantonese population in the United States. While many Chinese immigrants worked on both of the North American coasts, some moved to Hawai'i to work in the sugar fields. Contract labor from China greatly increased the number of Cantonese in the islands. A Chinese theater was built in the late 1870s in the heart of Chinatown to provide entertainment for local audiences, and Cantonese opera began to prosper in Hawai'i. Cantonese opera also developed in New York and San Francisco, but differently from the situation in Honolulu. Upon close examination subtle differences become apparent in the way Cantonese opera developed in Hawai'i.

Honolulu's Chinatown was established in the 1870s. The local center of Chinese commerce, Chinatown also functioned as a center of cultural and recreational activities. Cantonese opera in Hawai'i not only catered to Chinese but also functioned as a community event for other ethnic groups in the islands. Unlike ethnic relationships in the continental United States, Hawaii's plantation culture resulted in a more amenable social climate between immigrants groups through proximity and inter-marriage. As a result of the relatively tolerant cultural environment, Cantonese opera in Hawai'i acquired a more positive image among non-Chinese than it had on the mainland. The following is a local news-paper announcement of a Cantonese opera performance in 1879:

> A great attraction will be presented shortly, that will no doubt eclipse all the theatre and circus show of the Western barbarians. A Chinese dramatic company is about to open and will give a season. It will be extremely interesting, as we learn that one of their plays extends a period of more than hundred years. The interludes consist of musical entertainment—principally gongs, cymbals, and firecrackers. (from the *Pacific Commercial Advertiser,* January 25, 1879, cited in Glick 1980: 148)

The announcement suggests that a demand and appreciation for pro-fessional Cantonese opera performance existed in Honolulu in the late nineteenth century. Because the major Chinese population in Hawai'i was Cantonese, Cantonese culture became the dominant Chinese cul-ture in the islands. Consequently, Cantonese opera was seen as Chinese music for a long time. Only with the recent arrival of Chinese immi-grants from all over China has the dominance of Cantonese music been challenged.

Unlike Chinese who immigrated to the continental United States and who endured overt discrimination, early Chinese immigrants to the king-dom of Hawai'i established themselves as an influential ethnic group toward the end of the late nineteenth century. Many regional associations, clan associations, and cultural clubs were formed, and they played a major role in maintaining facets of Chinese culture in the islands. Among these cultural organizations were amateur Cantonese opera clubs, which were run by Cantonese music enthusiasts. The earliest club was established in the early 1900s. The Ching Wan (established in 1948) and Wo Lok (established in 1972) clubs are considered the most established. Both are still active. The Hua Xia (established in 1990; Figure 6.1) and Zi Jin (established in 2002) clubs are more recent additions that have attracted newer immigrants.

Although two of the New York clubs were established in the 1930s, Cantonese music clubs were not as popular in New York as in Hawai'i because many early immigrants to the city had to work long hours and had no leisure time. It was not until the 1980s when another wave of Chinese immigrants brought a group of Cantonese performers from Hong Kong and China to New York that Cantonese opera clubs really began to flourish. Because each of these Chinese communities was established by Cantonese people, Cantonese opera was perceived by insiders as Chinese music rather than as regional music. This ethnocentricity as well as limited exposure to other kind of Chinese musics

FIGURE 6.1 *Picture of the Honolulu Cantonese Opera club Hua Xia. Facing the two singers are musicians playing (from left) the gaohu, yangqin, and zhonghu. A zhong ruan player and the percussion session were in the back of the room and are not shown here. 2003. (Courtesy of Frederick Lau)*

indirectly influenced outsiders also to view Cantonese opera as representative of all Chinese music.

Expressing "Chaozhouness" in Thailand.   People from China have been in Thailand since the thirteenth century. However, many migrated to Thailand in great numbers in the sixteenth and seventeenth centuries and later in the nineteenth century mainly for economic reasons; most came from coastal regions such as Chaozhou, Fujian, Hakka, Canton, and Hainan (Figure 1.2). Those who left Chaozhou, by far the largest group, were businessmen and skilled agricultural workers. Within a short time they began to dominate the rice milling business in Bangkok (Skinner 1957: 214). By the mid-twentieth century, Chaozhou businessmen had become key players in the Thai economy and business. Their wealth provided them with special social status, which in turn created opportunities for them to sponsor events that highlighted their Chinese heritage and origins. Chinese cultural practice and expressions such as music, performing arts, and language school became important channels through which Chinese identity was maintained and expressed.

> **ACTIVITY 6.1**   *Go to the Internet and construct a brief history of the Chinese in Thailand. What kind of Chinese language was spoken among the different ethnic groups in Thailand? How did these early immigrants maintain their sense of identity, and what kinds of political hurdles did they have to overcome during the first part of the twentieth century?*

When I was conducting research in the late 1990s in Thailand, I found a number of amateur music clubs practicing Chaozhou music in Bangkok, the capital of Thailand (Figure 6.2). Members of these clubs perform Chaozhou instrumental music for their own enjoyment and to affirm their Chaozhou identity. During their practice, they demonstrate a strong sense of Chaozhou influence in many aspects of their activities. This is reflected in the language, conversation, and even snacks and tea, as well as in music and performance practice.

While privileging their Chaozhou identity, many club members describe their musical practice as derived from the Confucian ideal of amateur music-making (chapter 5). This concept is clearly shown in the clubs' names. Of the many music clubs I visited, the names of two clubs in particular caught my attention. The club Nanxun Sizhushe adopted

FIGURE 6.2 *Chaozhou club in Thailand. From left:* zhonghu, erxian, gehu, *percussion,* dizi, *and* yangqin. *1994. (Courtesy of Frederick Lau)*

its name from a music club that existed in Chaozhou, China, in the early twentieth century. The other group is Yeyun Ruyuexuan Quyituan—literally, "leaf melody Confucian music chamber and singing group." The direct reference to the Confucian ideal in the club's endeavor is clear. The imagery of "melody" and "leaf " reflects not only the owner's literary background but also his poetic aspiration and overall understanding of elite Chinese culture.

Members of these clubs are mostly middle-age second- or third-generation Chinese-Thai of Chaozhou heritage. The music they perform is Chaozhou *xianshiyue* ("music for strings of Chaozhou") and Chaozhou opera, two of the most popular genres in the Chaozhou region in China (CD track 12). Men perform exclusively Chaozhou instrumental music, perhaps a legacy of the Confucian ideology that dictates that playing of instruments is a male activity. Consequently, women's role in music was confined only to singing and in this case mostly excerpts from Chaozhou operas. The clubs usually own musical instruments that are typical in Chaozhou music ensembles. These include the characteristic two-stringed bowed lute *erxian* (Figure 1.14), the leading instrument in a *xianshi* ensemble, and an assortment of bowed and plucked strings such as the *erhu, pipa, yangqin,* and *sanxian* (see chapter 2). *Erxian* leads the music and is the most demanding instrument. Only skilled and respected musicians are invited to play it.

In a typical session, musicians gather at the club and wait for their turn. They spontaneously decide on the pieces and what instruments to play. The goal in these sessions is to be able to play a piece with the true flavor of the Chaozhou style and sensibility. Musicians consult commercial recordings from China when they have questions about styles and the music. For them the aesthetic essence is to sound like musicians in Chaozhou, which they consider as authentic style. The musicians I observed disliked the modern style and avoided it. In short, their approach to music is preservationist in nature and based on their memory of the past.

Chinese Music Singaporean Style.   Different from those types performed by Thai-Chinese, the Chinese music practiced in Singapore exemplifies another facet of Chineseness as defined by its multicultural and multiethnic social conditions. Of the roughly 4.5 million inhabitants of Singapore (2006 estimate), 76.8 percent are Chinese, 13.9 percent Malay, 7.9 percent Indian, and 1.4 percent other (percentages from 2000 census). However, the concept of being Chinese varies within the Chinese community. Some trace their ethnic ties back to a specific region in China although they may have never been there. Others downplay their Chinese roots completely and see themselves as Singaporeans. For the government, the concept of Chineseness is based upon a pan-Chinese model that collapses all regional and dialect groups into a generic category for the sake of national unity. Thus, the Chinese music that has been officially promoted is modern in outlook like modernized traditional music that is not associated with specific regional groups.

The Singaporean Chinese Orchestra is richly funded by the government and it performs repertory similar to what is performed in China. In fact, many players were originally from China. Their repertory tends to be music popularized in contemporary China and other Chinese-speaking countries.

ACTIVITY 6.2   *The Singapore Chinese Orchestra and the Hong Kong Chinese Orchestra are two important Chinese orchestras in Asia. Strongly supported by the government, each orchestra* *is unique in it presentation, programming, and musical direction. Examine the websites of both orchestras and compare how they are different in terms of their organization and activity. Based on this information, write an essay on the image and identity of these two groups.*

But outside the official cultural structure, the situation is quite different. The various different Chinese communities organize music activities that are based on their regional affiliations. Depending on the place of origin, the kind of Chinese music changes from group to group. Among Chinese from Fujian province, *nanguan* music is considered the most important genre. Fujian associations devote a lot of effort to the preservation and performance of *nanguan*. The most important *nanguan* music club in Singapore is the Siong Leng Musical Association, whose members are heavily involved in promoting *nanguan* music to the general public and younger audiences. They put on public performances for outreach and have even published a book outlining the history of *nanguan* in Singapore.

However, among the Chaozhou Chinese circle, the situation is somewhat different. The two most prominent Chaozhou music clubs in Singapore have been Er Woo Amateur Music & Dramatic Association (hereafter Er Woo) and Thau Yong Amateur Musical Association (hereafter Thau Yong). Established by Chaozhou immigrants in the early twentieth century, these two clubs were set up to promote Chaozhou culture and to create a social network for Chaozhou immigrants in Singapore.

Er Woo, or Yu Yu Yuyueshe (Confucian Music Association), is the oldest amateur music club in Singapore (Figure 6.3). Established in 1912 by a group of Chaozhou businessmen, Er Woo's primary focus was to promote music of the Hakka region known as Hanju (*Han* opera) and *handiao* (Hakka instrumental music). As a form of leisure and artistic pursuit that conformed to the Confucian ideal of spiritual enlightenment through music-making, this type of regional music was popularized in China among the local Chaozhou elitist literati of the time. Later, they also began to perform Chaozhou music, despite its once having been viewed as music of low-class status. With the help of teachers from China, Er Woo's reputation blossomed. Between 1928 and 1935, Er Woo was contracted by several European record companies, such as Pathe, Beke, Orion, Columbia, and Victor, to make recordings of the *hanju* opera for the burgeoning phonograph market in Southeast Asia. Er Woo's activities resumed after World War II. It continued to present Hanju and later to produce full-length Chaozhou opera as well.

Along with Er Woo, Thau Yong is remembered as one of a handful of music clubs that has exerted strong musical influence on Chinese music in Singapore. The club was established by members who left Er Woo because they disagreed with the formality and class consciousness of the Er Woo members. Thau Yong presented itself as a group for the commoners. The goal of Thau Yong was to provide a context in which its members could perform *hanju* (opera from the Hakka region) and to counteract Er Woo's elitist approach in accepting members.

In the late 1950s, Thau Yong began to expand its activities to include arrangements of traditional Chinese instrumental music for Chinese orchestra. This music is similar to the modernized traditional music that the post-1949 government tried to promote in the PRC. With a growing membership in 1959, it formed the first Chinese orchestra in Singapore. Thau Yong was a pioneer in promoting this kind of modernized Chinese music in addition to its routine of performing *hanju* opera.

FIGURE 6.3   *Picture of the Singapore amateur music club Er Woo. Notice the use of a collection of Chinese instruments with the addition of a cello. From left:* gu, suona, cello, dizi, *and* yangqin. *(Courtesy of Frederick Lau)*

In recognizing the importance of recruiting younger players to continue the tradition, Thau Yong also began to offer instrumental classes such as *pipa, sanxian,* and *guzheng* to younger players in 1957. Since then, Thau Yong has divided its focus between both *hanju* and Chinese instrumental music, in which Er Woo has not been interested. Its promotion of PRC musical ideology was considered by the government as politically motivated and pro-communist; therefore its activities were under close scrutiny by officials. Consequently, club activities were halted in the late 1950s. They were resumed in the mid-1960s after Singapore gained independence.

In the late 1960s, Chinese music activities and politics became disassociated through the establishment of Singapore as a multicultural and multiethnic nation-state. Playing in these amateur music clubs became acceptable and desirable to the public, and the government also saw this kind of musical activity as a way to reaffirm the nationalist commitment to a multicultural society. The Singaporean government began to provide financial support for Chinese music activities. For example, in 1968 under the auspices of the Minister of Culture, the government established a Chinese orchestra as part of the National Theater, and it became a professional orchestra in 1974. In 1992 this group was officially changed to the Singapore Chinese Orchestra and in 1996 it was further changed to the Singapore National Chinese Orchestra. It is interesting to note that China's "national music" has morphed to become an important component of Singapore's "national music." Clearly the overall political climate has changed drastically since the early days of Er Woo and Thau Yong.

With a favorable environment for Chinese music, amateur music clubs became more active. Both Er Woo and Thau Yong have given many public performances of full-length Chaozhou opera with impressive financial support from their members and business sponsors. Their musical focus, which is different from that of earlier times, has shifted to Chaozhou opera and Chaozhou instrumental music; *hanju,* the previous music of choice, is rarely performed. This shift signifies not only the prominence of Chaozhou people in Singapore society but also a growing demand for Chaozhou music and culture. Officials from the Ministry of Culture are often present during these performances to endorse these events and reaffirm the government's commitment to this type of cultural performance. The success of these performances is a far cry from the days when playing Chinese music was suspicious in the eyes of the government and an icon only for Chaozhou elite. Formerly only valued by its participants as a marker of their Chinese regional identity, Chaozhou music is now an important cultural ingredient of multiethnic and multicultural Singapore.

CIRCULATION OF POPULAR MUSIC
OF VARIOUS SORTS

Jon Jang, the Chinese Jazzman.   Known in America as a jazz musician, composer, and pianist, Jon Jang has established himself as a strong voice in Asian American music. Born in Los Angeles in 1954 of Chinese descent, Jon and his two siblings were raised by their single mother in Palo Alto. He began playing the piano at the age of nineteen and eventually graduated from Oberlin Conservatory of Music with a B.A. degree in piano performance. Eclectic in style, Jon Jang's music mixes idioms of jazz, Chinese music, and European classical music that reflect his background and Chinese American identity. Being a second generation Chinese American, he is keenly aware of the Chinese immigration experience in the United States and often works it into his compositions. CD track 50, entitled "Two Flowers on a Stem" (1994), is one such work. According to Jang, the title is a "metaphor expressing the symbiotic relationship of his cultural identity and musical aesthetics as an American born Chinese":

> During the 90s, I had been listening to Chinese folk songs, from both northern and southern regions of China. When I was creating "Two Flowers on a Stem," I composed a melody for the *erhu* that had characteristics very similar to Chinese folk songs, but I placed it in my own context. I wanted to compose a love song that would allow conflict to become tenderness, to express a desire for beauty and strength. When I heard Jiebing Chen's *erhu* performance in the fall of 1994, it was the voice penetrating the heart of tragedy and transforming it into the embodiment of beauty. There is a strong connection in the relationship between tragedy and beauty that can be traced to the works by early composers for the *erhu*. Hua Yanjun [aka, "Blind" Abing] began his early life as an orphan and lived in a life of poverty. When he began to lose his sight, he composed "Moon Reflected over the Autumn Lake" as a way to remember the beauty of life....One of the personal meanings behind "Two Flowers on a Stem" is about adopting Chinese music in my musical language and a daughter from China in my life. This period in my life showed how tragedy can turn into beauty, "when sorrow turns to joy." (http://www.jonjang. com/two_flowers/)

ACTIVITY 6.3 *In the brief excerpt of Jon Jang's music on CD track 50, you should be able to hear the familiar sound of a Chinese chordophone. Can you identify it? While listening to it, pay close attention to the accompaniment to the main melody. How it is similar to or different from other Chinese music examples you have previously heard in this book?*

Mandarin Song-Singing Clubs. Chaozhou *xianshi* music is not the only form of Chinese music played by amateur musicians in Thailand. During my subsequent trips, I came across another musical activity that has become a favorite among urban Thai-Chinese in the last decade. Many urbanites preferred singing Chinese popular songs in singing clubs and public venues to other traditional music activities, such as playing Chaozhou music and opera. A major influence in the popularization of modern Chinese songs in Thailand was the radio, a trend that began after mid-1954. Radio broadcast a number of musical genres, including popular and traditional Chinese music. Apart from hearing many kinds of regional and traditional music on the radio, many Thai-Chinese were exposed to more modern and diverse Chinese music. Consequently, the practice of singing Mandarin popular songs began to flourish among the younger generations who had learned to speak Mandarin in Chinese schools in Thailand.

While most people in Thailand and other Chinese diasporic communities usually speak in one or more regional dialects such as Cantonese, Chaozhouese, Hakka, or Hainanese, those who attended local Chinese schools are also able to speak Mandarin, the only language taught in Chinese schools. Being able to speak Mandarin marks a person's level of education, personal history, social status, and age.

With the help of gramophone records and cassette recordings beginning in the 1960s, people were able to learn Mandarin popular songs easily. Singing these songs became one of the most popular pastimes for many middle-class Thai-Chinese. As a result, the number of Chinese singing studios, singing clubs, and choral groups in Bangkok has proliferated since the 1990s. The majority of the songs sung at the clubs are those popularized between the 1960s and 1980s (Figure 6.4).

At present, singing Mandarin songs has replaced many traditional forms of entertainment and music-making, such as regional Chinese opera, storytelling, and instrumental music. Mandarin songs remind

FIGURE 6.4 *Singing club in Thailand. 1995. (Courtesy of Frederick Lau)*

the singers and audiences of their youth when these songs were extremely popular. Club members consider these songs to be a vital part of Chinese culture with which they can identify.

In the 1990s, amateur singing clubs blossomed because they were relatively informal and easy to establish. Most of these clubs hold their sessions in public spaces such as public parks, regional associations, community centers, classrooms, or recreation halls. All that is needed is a mobile unit that houses an amplifier, speakers, and a machine that plays prerecorded accompaniments. Clubs are open to participants of all ages but are mostly frequented by adults between the age of thirty and seventy. Male and female members mingle freely in these clubs. The atmosphere and behavior during a session is social, casual, and festive, like a group of old friends getting together to have a good time (CD track 51).

Members usually pay a membership fee to join, regardless of their singing ability, gender, and regional affiliation. To sing in commercially operated clubs, members pay for each song they sing in addition to a nominal membership fee. In each session, singers take turns singing, and each singer can usually sing two to three songs, depending on the number of singers present. Most clubs hire a singing coach to come in once a week. The songs have symbolic importance and value for individuals and communities in Thai-Chinese society because they capture a sense of Chineseness that allows Thai-Chinese to see themselves as modern. Considering the songs' relationship to the people who sang them, the history of Chinese in Thailand, and the current social climate, it is not difficult to understand why Mandarin songs continue to enjoy popularity in today's singing clubs.

Chinese Chorus and Singing/Karaoke beyond Asia.   I have shown earlier that singing popular Chinese songs has become a popular activity amongst Thai-Chinese. However, this activity is not limited to Thailand. Singing Chinese songs has risen to prominence in a number of diasporic Chinese communities. Formal and informal Chinese choruses, singing clubs, and Chinese song contests have become standard fare in many overseas Chinese communities. Many cities, such as Houston, San Jose, Honolulu, Chicago, New York, and Boston, have Chinese choirs, as do many universities with large Chinese student populations (Figure 6.5). The mission for many of the groups is to promote Chinese choral music, enhance the level of appreciation of Chinese culture, provide educational programs for those who are interested in Chinese culture and Mandarin language, and establish a network for members of their communities. Through singing Chinese songs, these groups foster cultural understanding and bridge the gap between Chinese and other ethnic groups in their social environment. In short, Mandarin songs became an effective cultural icon for affirming and communicating their Chinese identity.

The songs they sing are mostly twentieth-century choral works composed by the first wave of Chinese composers who adopted Western music in the first half of the twentieth century. Often written for a mixed voice, four-part choir, these songs are composed by mixing traditional Chinese and European musical elements. As the popularity of choral singing grew, schools across China adopted choral singing into their music curriculums. Because of the popular appeal of choral singing, choral pieces were also used for protests and political rallies. Many famous revolutionary mass songs (see chapter 5) were composed during this period. In fact, the 1930s–1950s has been considered the golden age of Chinese choral music and many of the pieces from this period are now considered classics. While the meanings of these songs have changed, these choral pieces continue to be associated with homeland and patriotic feeling toward China and occupy a special place in diasporic communities. Thus, the Chinese

FIGURE 6.5 *San Jose Chinese Choir (top) and Honolulu Han Sheng Choir (bottom) taken during a public concert in 2004. (Courtesy of Frederick Lau)*

choir is a site in which singers articulate their memory and love for the homeland, as well as nostalgia for the place of origin that they have not visited. Chinese choirs usually hold regular practice and perform at major Chinese functions such as Chinese New Year Celebration, Mid-Autumn Festival, National Days, Chinese Community Events, and local charity functions.

CD track 52 is a typical Chinese choral work. The lyrics are written in Chinese and the music is based on the musical style of nineteenth-century European music, a popular compositional style typical of most choral pieces written in the last several decades. As in most Chinese choral pieces, the accompaniment is played by the piano and based on chords and harmony. This piece, entitled "Exiting the Border," depicts the singer's emotional state of mind when leaving the country. The first verse of the song is as follows:

Please sing me an exiting-the-border song	*Qingweiwo changyishou chu sai qu*
Using that ancient language	*Yongna yiwang de gulao yanyu*
Please use that beautiful vibrato	*Qingyong meili de chanyin*
To gently call my beautiful country	*Qingqing huhuan woxinzhong de dahao heshan*

The lyrics glorify love for the mother country and the memory of the beautiful river and pasture that one leaves behind. Like this one, many other songs written since the 1930s contain themes about the homeland, nostalgia, love, and patriotic sentiments to arouse the spirit of the people. This also underscores the important social function of choral music, especially during mass gatherings and rallies. On rare occasions, other regional dialects will be used depending on the origin of the piece.

Although most choral pieces are sung in Mandarin, in recent years songs sung in regional dialects are getting increasingly popular inside and outside China. In 2003, the *China Daily* reported that a Fujian dialect song contest was held in mid-September. The contest stipulated that all contestants were Chinese who were originally from southern Fujian province, including those from Taiwan province, Canada, Malaysia, and Singapore. The headline read "Dialect Song Contest Brings Together People across Taiwan Straits." Obviously an intention of this contest was to use songs to unite people according to their place of origin. The first contest of its kind, it attracted more than one thousand domestic and inter-national participants who speak the Minnan dialect, the dialect of southern Fujian in southeastern China. Since over 80 percent of Taiwanese are descended from southern Fujian people, and many Chinese in Malaysia,

Singapore, and the Philippines share the same culture and language as southern Fujian locals, this contest was created to promote regional identity through songs of the Fujian region. This contest reaffirms that regional identity is a driving force in Chinese identity. This also explains why popular songs sung in Fujian dialects have a big market in places where Fujian dialect and identity are prominent.

In 2004, an international Chinese singing contest was held in Kuala Lumpur in Malaysia with participants from most English-speaking countries in the West. Most of the songs were Mandarin songs from Taiwan and Hong Kong. What is significant about these events is the widespread practice of singing Chinese songs for the purpose of identifying and affirming Chinese identity, whether pan-Chinese or regional.

At a less formal level, singing Chinese songs in karaoke style is popular in many Chinese communities across the world. I have attended numerous karaoke-singing sessions organized by Chinese groups in San Francisco and Honolulu. Casey Lum's detailed study of karaoke in New York City sheds lights on the intention and motivation of singing karaoke as an activity among friends. Many migrants use karaoke as a way of participating in a community (Lum 1996: 36). As a new media, karaoke offers an affordable alternative to singing operatic songs with live instrumental accompaniments. It also produces results beyond social, economic, and musical concerns. Singing karaoke creates community within groups, and this symbolic act also establishes a bond that reinforces Cantonese identity and, for many, a specific Hong Kong or southern Chinese sense of being. In fusing traditional musical practices with new technology, overseas Chinese have found another viable outlet in which to exercise their creativity and renew their ethnic ties. As Lum insightfully states, "Through imaginative uses, karaoke is adopted to create unique cultural experiences by combining traditional theatrical forms, new media, and cultural practices in the diaspora" (Lum 1996: 53).

ACTIVITY 6.4 *Try to locate a commercial karaoke singing establishment in your town. Join with a few friends and survey its song list to see if the establishment offers Chinese songs. If so, choose one or two to sing and as you do, take note of the text and musical characteristics. One of you should listen for instrumentation, another for the characteristics of the melody, another for the text content. Then discuss how you would place that song among the types of Chinese music written about in this book.*

Something New, Something Old: Chinese Music at a Crossroad.

When Twelve Girls get together East meets West as the Twelve Girls
Band performs traditional tunes and remakes of contemporary songs.
The ensemble's sound dates back more than 1,500 years with its use
of instruments such as the dizi *(bamboo flute),* guzheng *(a zither with*
movable frets) and four-stringed pipa *lute. Add in electronic keyboards*
and pulsating percussion for a modern twist on age-old sounds.

Honolulu Advertiser (*October, 28, 2005*)

I now turn to a recent trend in Chinese music that has catered to audiences outside China. This genre of music is characterized by a fusion of traditional music with contemporary pop music sounds performed by an all-female ensemble (CD track 53). Developed first for Japanese audiences, this crossover style gained widespread popularity in Asia and the United States and eventually made its way back to China. This contemporary Chinese music is not without controversy. Some critics charge that it presents a false image to audiences and that it undermines the integrity of Chinese music. Supporters claim that traditional Chinese music should not be kept in a museum and that this kind of music helps to revitalize declining interest. This debate brings to the fore a fundamental question having to do with defining traditional Chinese music. For this discussion, I will focus on the group called Twelve Girls Band (TGB; Figure 6.6).

FIGURE 6.6 *Twelve Girls Band. From left: two* erhu, guzheng *(back),* pipa, dizi, guzheng *(back),* pipa, dizi, pipa, guzheng *(back), and two* erhu. (*Courtesy of Frederick Lau*)

TGB is an all-women's performing group formed in Beijing on June 1, 2001, by Wang Xiaojing, former manager of the rock star Cui Jian (see chapter 4). When it was first formed, it targeted the international market. It was little known within China. TGB's reputation grew drastically only after it gave its debut concert, "Beautiful Energy," in Japan in 2003. The band consists of twelve young and attractive traditional instrumentalists, all of whom are graduates of top music conservatories in China. The featured Chinese instruments include *pipa, erhu, yangqin, guzheng,* and *dizi.* TGB's music is, as one press release describes, an "exotic, yet accessible sound and an instrumental repertoire which includes tunes familiar to Western audiences" (http://starbulletin.com/2004/09/03/features/story6.html). The main attractions of TGB are its glitzy image, innovative stage presence, and creative presentation/combination of a number of Chinese traditional instruments with contemporary music sound and features.

According to the Wang Xiaojing, the aim of TGB is "to internationalize Chinese traditional music." Rather than relying on the conventions in performing traditional music, TGB's music has undergone what he calls "modern commercial packaging." The musical treatment includes adding an underlying rock beat, amplified instruments, a synthesizer, percussion, and a variety of electronic sounds, as well as an unapologetic use of music clichés borrowed from Western pop and classical music. All players, including those on *erhu, yangqin,* and *guzheng,* perform standing up. This is a major departure from traditional performance practice. According to Wang, TGB's music is "not traditional music, nor is it popular music, it is whatever people want to make of it" (Chen 2004).

Like performers in pop music, TGB members pay close attention to their image and presentation. While TGB's image is constantly refreshing and innovative, it comprises the selective use of Chinese elements. To this end, the selection of their players, according to their website, is based not only on their techniques but also on their figures and beautiful smiles. The format of TGB is derived from the concept of *yuefan,* a Tang dynasty court practice of having an all-women ensemble perform to entertain guests. The ensemble's job was to provide music and beauty for their audiences.

The name of the group is based on the number 12, which is considered a lucky number in Chinese cosmology. According to Wang, "Just as there are 12 months in a year, 12 animals in the Chinese zodiac, and 12 golden hairpins that represent womanhood in Chinese lore, 12 was the lucky number that would help the group to conquer the world."

Despite Wang's disclaimer that TGB is not about traditional music, TGB is self-consciously playing with and off Chinese traditional music elements and using Chinese icons as a marketing ploy. The following media highlights are representative of how TGB has been portrayed in the press and has been received by critics:

> "World shrinks for 12"...Like many crossover acts with international appeal, Twelve Girls Band has earned converts through an exotic, yet accessible sound and an instrumental repertoire which includes tunes familiar to Western audiences....Having sold more than 2 million copies of their debut album in Japan alone and scoring a platinum follow-up, the multi-instrumentalist ensemble now has its sights set on the rest of the world. (*Honolulu Star Bulletin,* http://starbulletin. com/2004/09/03/features/story6.html)

> There's something mesmerizing about the band's graceful stage presence, their technical virtuosity—and most of all, their euphoric expressions as they play their instruments. (*Time Magazine,* http:// www.uapresents.org/press/press_releases.php?id=1855)

The majority of the press releases emphasize recurring phrases such as "1500 years of Chinese tradition," "East-West blending," and "crossover genre." Whatever the reason is behind TGB's success, it is noteworthy that this group has a big following in Japan, and its popularity at home rose only after TGB made it big in Japan. This trend may suggest that China's recent popular culture is as influenced by the Japanese present as it is by the Chinese past.

In terms of their musical style, TGB performs in an intense, unconventional, and high-energy fashion, making the complex arrangements appear effortless. Their music is laden with pop-performance standards: It is upbeat, with a fast rhythm, exaggerated body movements, and unrelenting smiles, all in orchestrated unity before a huge backdrop of projected colorful laser images in a variety of geometric patterns. With traditional Chinese instruments, TGB's music is a fusion of Chinese instrumental cliché with synthesized, poplike, fast-paced rhythms. Pieces usually consist of an alternation of solo versus group tutti accompanied by a drum beat and electronic percussion. CD track 53 is an opening of one of the leading songs on their album *Beautiful Energy.* As critic Jackie Lam wrote after TGB's UCLA performance: "With their synchronized bopping heads, furiously moving mallets and infectious energy, the vibrant twenty-somethings from the PRC mix the modern with the traditional bounded in a seamless musical embrace" (Lam 2004).

Whether one likes this kind of music or not, TGB has created a new approach in performing traditional music. Its music is based on a cosmopolitan sensibility that erases any trace of obvious connection to specific regional style or sound. Accentuated by heavy rock 'n roll beats and rhythmic drives, this music cannot be easily pigeonholed. Because of the players and the use of Chinese instruments, most non-Chinese audiences label it Chinese music. However, TGB's presentation is imagined as cosmopolitanism and marketed as global music. The future of this innovative use of traditional music remains to be seen.

CONCLUSION

In participating in the variety of "Chinese" music being produced beyond China in recent decades, performers and composers have drawn their creative inspirations from idealized and imaginary notions of Chineseness. Their musical expressions are closely intertwined with the identity politics and external societal forces of their new contexts. While there are certain sonic resemblances between the new musics and those produced inside China, Chinese music in the international context has transformed into something quite different from its roots. As China continues to redefine its "national music," so will musicians who live and work outside the country.

In this book, I have presented three themes for better understanding the processes that have shaped Chinese music: ideology, identity, and modernization. These three themes have mingled through time to produce the dominant forces in the production, perpetuation, and definition of Chinese music. What I have shown in these chapters is that the term *Chinese music* is multifaceted rather than a single and static entity. To talk meaningfully about Chinese music requires specifying a particular form of music and considering it in relation to historical, political, regional, and other cultural contexts. Music continues to be a dynamic part of Chinese culture, one that reflects the complexity of Chineseness over time and around the globe.

Glossary

Aerophone Instrument whose primary sound medium is a vibrating air column.

Atonal Music without a tonal center or tonality.

Avant-garde A musical style that emerged in the early part of the twentieth century as a reaction to music written in the nineteenth-century Romantic style.

Badaqu The eight big pieces in *jiangnan sizhu* repertory.

Chaozhou An area in northeastern Guangdong province. The language and customs of this region are closer to those of Fujian province than those of Guangdong.

Chuida Wind and percussion ensemble.

Chordophone Instrument whose primary sound medium is a vibrating string.

Chou Clown or comic character in Beijing opera.

Confucianism Teaching and ideology of the scholar and philosopher Confucius of the Warring period (475–221 B.C.). His philosophy of society and relationship has been influential in China, Japan, and Korea.

Da hou Literally, "big voice," sung by a martial male role in Cantonese opera.

Dan Young female in *Chinese* opera.

Daoism An indigenous Chinese philosophy and religion. As a philosophy, it advocates nonaggression, noninterference, and natural ways of life. As a folk religion, Daoism is a form of mysticism that aims to control an esoteric way of accessing the sources of all cosmological processes or path, called *dao,* by means of alchemy, chant, and ritual.

Difang yinyue Regional music.

Dizi Side-blown bamboo flute with a membrane placed between the blow hole and the first finger hole.

Equal-tempered tuning A tuning system in which the octave is divided into twelve equal parts. This tuning is used on modern pianos.

Erhu Two-stringed fretless bowed fiddle that is held vertically. The bow sits between the two strings that are tuned a fifth apart.

Errentai A song-and-dance style popularized in the Shannxi province and Inner Mongolia.

Fazhan Development.

Gewutuan Song and dance troupe.

Glissando Sliding from one pitch to the next.

Guoyue Music of the nation.

Guzheng Twelve- or thirteen-stringed plucked zither.

Heterophony One melody performed in slightly different versions simultaneously.

Jiangnan sizhu Regional instrumental genre popularized in East Central China. Literally, "silk and bamboo" music from south of the Yangtze River.

Jing Painted face character in *Beijing* opera.

Laodan Old woman character in *Beijing* opera.

Longzhou Cantonese vocal genre; literally, "dragon boat."

Kexuehua Scientific.

Membranophone Instrument whose primary sound medium is a vibrating membrane.

Minjian Literally, "among the folk." It refers to unofficial "folk" practices that are outside those censored by government-sponsored or official institutions.

Minyue Traditional music.

Minyuetuan Traditional music orchestra.

Minzu yinyue Music of the people or nation.

Modulation Change of one tonal center or key to another.

Nanyin Cantonese vocal narrative genre usually accompanied by the plucked-string *sanxian*.

Ping hou Ordinary voice in Cantonese opera singing.

Pipa Four-stringed pear-shaped fretted plucked lute. Its Japanese equivalent is the *biwa*.

Qinqin Two-stringed fretted plucked lute with a narrow neck and a small hexagonal resonator.

Sanxian Unfretted three-stringed plucked lute with a small rectangular resonator covered by snakeskin.

Suyue Secular music.

Sheng Mouth organ capable of producing more than one pitch. The Japanese counterpart is the *sho*. Also refers to a young male in Beijing opera.

Strophic songs Songs in which the same melody is set to multiple verses that are separated by a chorus or refrain.

Tablature A form of music notation that gives playing instruction instead of pitch and rhythm.

Timbre Tone sound.

Tongsu gequ Popularized songs.

Wenyi wanhui Evening cultural show.

Xiao Vertical bamboo notched flute with six to eight finger holes.

Xianshi String ensemble from Chaozhou area in southern China. Literally, "string and poetry."

Xiqu Opera and theater.

Yangge Field song, a type of folk song from northwestern China.

Yangqin Chinese hammered dulcimer with a range of three to four octaves, usually played with a pair of bamboo beaters.

Yangyue Western music.

Yaogun yinyue Rock and roll music.

Yayue Elegant court music.

Yinyue Music.

Yiren Professional artist.

Yuegong Music labor or craftsman.

Yueqin Three-stringed short-necked fretted lute with a flat round resonator.

Zi hou Refers to a woman's voice that sounds like that of a boy in Cantonese opera singing.

Zhonghu Slightly larger version of the *erhu* and tuned slightly lower.

Zhuanye A contemporary term referring to someone who is a professional and specialist.

References

Allen, Joseph Roe. 1992. *In the voice of others: Chinese Music Bureau poetry.* Ann Arbor: Center for Chinese Studies, University of Michigan.

Baranovitch, Nimrod. 2003. *China's new voices: Popular music, ethnicity, gender, and politics, 1978–1997.* Berkeley: University of California Press.

Chang, Chi-jen. 1983. Alexander Tcherepnin, his influence on modern Chinese music. In program booklet of the memorial concert *Tcherepnin and China* presented by the Foundation for Chinese Performing Arts Inc. on November 30, 1992, Sanders Theatre, Harvard University.

Chan, Sauyan. 1997. *Shidi kaocha yu xiqu yanjiu (Field research and the study of opera).* Hong Kong: Cantonese Opera Research Project, Chinese University of Hong Kong.

Chen, Bing. 2004. Why is the Twelve Girls Band famous? Because they modernize traditional music? *China Daily.* URL: http://big5.xinhuanet.com/gate/big5/news.xinhuanet.com/audio/2004-03/01/content_1337904.htm

Chou, Wen-Chung. 1969. Towards a re-merger in music. In *Contemporary Composers on Contemporary Music,* E. Schwarz and B. Childs. New York: Da Capo Press, 308–315.

———. 1971. Asian concepts and twentieth-century western composers. *Musical Quarterly* LVII(2): 211–229.

———. 1977. Asian and western music: Influence of confluence? *Asian Culture Quarterly* 5: 60–66.

DeWoskin, Kenneth. 1982. *A Song for one or two: Music and the concept of art in early China.* Ann Arbor: Center for Chinese Studies, University of Michigan.

Duara, Prasenjit. 1995. *Rescuing history from the nation: Questioning narratives of modern China.* Chicago: The University of Chicago Press.

Falkenhausen, Lothar von. 1993. *Suspended music: Chime-bells in the culture of Bronze Age China.* Berkeley: University of California Press.

Glick, Clarence Elmer. 1980. *Sojourners and settlers, Chinese migrants in Hawaii.* Honolulu: University Press of Hawaii.

Goldstein, Joshua. 1999. Mei Lanfang and the nationalization of Peking Opera, 1912–1930. *Positions* 7(2): 377–420.

Gramsci, Antonio. 1971. *Selections from the prison notebooks of Antonio Gramsci.* Edited and translated by Quintin Hoare and Geoffrey Smith. New York: International Publishers.

Gulik, R. H. van. 1969. *The lore of the Chinese lute.* Tokyo, and Rutland, VT: The Charles E. Tuttle Company.

Guy, Nancy. 1999. Governing the arts, governing the state: Peking Opera and political authority in Taiwan. *Ethnomusicology* 43(3): 508–526.

―――. 2005. *Peking opera and politics in Taiwan.* Urbana: University of Illinois Press.

Han, Kuo-Huang. 1978. The Chinese concept of program music. *Asian Music* X(1): 17–38.

―――. 1979. The modern Chinese orchestra. *Asian Music* XI(1): 1–43.

Ho, Wai-Chung. 2000. The political meaning of Hong Kong popular music: A review of sociopolitical relations between Hong Kong and the People's Republic of China since the 1980s. *Popular Music* 19(3): 341–353.

Jones, Andrew F. 1992. *Like a knife: Ideology and genre in contemporary Chinese popular music.* Ithaca, NY: East Asia Program, Cornell University.

―――. 2001. *Yellow music: Media culture and colonial modernity in the Chinese jazz age.* Durham, NC: Duke University Press.

Kloet, Jeroen de. 2000. Let him fucking see the green smoke beneath my groin—The mythology of Chinese rock. In *Postmodernism and China,* edited by A. Dirlik and X. Zhang. Durham, NC: Duke University Press.

Kraus, Richard. 1989. *Pianos and politics in China: Middle-class ambitions and the struggle over western music.* New York and Oxford: Oxford University Press.

Lam, Joseph. 1994. Notational representation and contextual constraints: How and why did Ye Tang notate his kun opera arias? In *Themes and variations: Writings on music in honor of Rulan Chao Pian,* edited by B. Yung and J. S. C. Lam. Cambridge, MA: Department of Music, Harvard University.

Lau, Frederick. 1996. Forever Red: The invention of solo *dizi* music in post-1949 China. *British Journal of Ethnomusicology* 5: 113–132.

―――. 1998. Packaging identity through sound: Tourist performances in contemporary China. *Journal of Musicological Research* 17: 113–134.

―――. 2004. Fusion or fission: The paradox and politics of contemporary Chinese avant-garde music. In *Locating East Asia in Western Art Music,* edited by Yayoi Uno Everett and Frederick Lau. Middletown, CT: Wesleyan University Press, 22–39.

Lee, Gregory. 1995. The "East is Red" goes pop: Commodification, hybridity and nationalism in Chinese popular song and its televisual performance. *Popular Music* 14(1): 95–110.

Lee, Leo Ou-fan. 1999. *Shanghai modern: The flowering of a new urban culture in China 1930–1945.* Cambridge, MA: Harvard University Press.

Lee, Robert G. 1999. *Orientals: Asian Americans in popular culture* (Asian American history and culture series). Philadelphia: Temple University Press.

Levenson, Joseph. 1957. The amateur ideal in Ming and early Ch'ing society: Evidence from painting. In *Chinese thought and institutions,* edited by J. Fairbank. Chicago: University of Chicago Press.

Li, Minxiong. 1987. *Minzu qiyue zhishi guangbo jiangzuo (Broadcast Lectures on the knowledge of national instrumental music).* Beijing: Renmin Yinyue Chubanshe (People's Yinyue Publishing Company).

Lum, Casey Man Kong. 1996. *In search of a voice: Karaoke and the construction of identity in Chinese America.* Mahwah, NJ: L. Erlbaum Associates.

McDougall, Bonnie. 1980. *Mao Zedong's talks at the Yan'an conference on literature and art.* Ann Arbor: Center for Chinese Studies, University of Michigan.

Moon, Krystyn R. 2005. *Yellowface: Creating the Chinese in American popular music and performance, 1850s–1920s.* New Brunswick, N.J.: Rutgers University Press.

Moys, James S. 1993. *Marginal sights: Staging the Chinese in America.* Iowa City: University of Iowa.

Pan-Chew, Shuhji. 2004. *Chou Wen-Chung music festival: Special album 2003.* Taipei, Taiwan: Canada–Taiwan Music & Arts Exchange.

Riddle, Ronald. 1983. *Flying dragons, flowing streams: Music in the life of San Francisco's Chinese.* Westport and London: Greenwood Press.

Skinner, G. William. 1957. *Chinese society in Thailand: An analytical history.* Ithaca, NY: Cornell University Press.

Stock, Jonathan. 1996. *Musical creativity in twentieth-century China.* Rochester, NY: University of Rochester Press.

Tchen, John Kuo Wei. 1999. *New York before Chinatown: Orientalism and the shaping of American culture, 1776–1882.* Baltimore, MD: Johns Hopkins University Press.

Wade, Bonnie C. 2005. *Music in Japan: Experiencing music, expressing culture.* New York: Oxford University Press.

Wang, Yuhe. 1984. *Zhongguo Jinxiandai Yinyueshi [A history of modern Chinese music].* Beijing: Renmin Yinyue Chubanshe [People's Music Publishing Company].

———. 1992. *Zhongguo Jinxiandai Yinyuejia pingzhuan [Critical biographies of modern Chinese musicians].* Beijing: Wenhua yishu Chubanshe [Culture and Arts Publishing Company].

Wong, Isabel. 1985. The many roles of Peking Opera in San Francisco in the 1980s. *UCLA Selected Reports in Ethnomusicology* 6: 173–188.

Yang, Mu. 1994. Academic ignorance or political taboo? Some issues in China's study of its folk song culture. *Ethnomusicology* 38/2: 303–320.

Ye, Dong. 1983. *Minzu qiyue de ticai yu xingshi* (*Types and forms of national instrumental music*). Shanghai: Shanghai Wenyi Chubanshe (Shanghai Arts Publishing Company).

Yu, Siuwah. 1996. *The meaning and cultural functions of non-Chinese music in the Eighteenth century Manchu Court.* Ph.D. Dissertation, Harvard University.

Yuan, Jingfang. 1987. *Minzu qiyue* (*National instrumental music*). Beijing: Renmin Yinyue Chubanshe (People's Music Publishing Company).

Yung, Bell. 1989. *Cantonese opera: Performance as creative process.* Cambridge: Cambridge University Press.

Yung, Bell, Evelyn Sakakida Rawski, and Rubie S. Watson, eds. 1996. *Harmony and counterpoint: Ritual music in Chinese context.* Stanford, CA: Stanford University Press.

Zheng, Su. 1994. Music making in cultural displacement: The Chinese-Asian odyssey. *Diaspora* 3(3): 273–288.

$Resources$

Bada geming xiandai yangbanxi [*Eight revolutionary modern yangbanxi*]. Video
  CD, China Records. ISRC CN-A01-98-0093-98, ISRC C10-00-0020-0/V.J8-9.

Chang, Peter M. 1991. Tan Dun's string quartet feng-ya-song: Some ideological issues. *Asian Music* 22(2): 127–158.

Crump, J. I., and William P. Malm, eds. 1975. *Chinese and Japanese music-
  dramas* (*Michigan papers in Chinese studies no. 19*). Ann Arbor: Center for
  Chinese Studies, University of Michigan.

Fang, Kun. 1981. A discussion on Chinese national musical traditions. *Asian
  Music* 12(2): 1–16.

Gao, Houyong. 1989. On qupai. *Asian Music* 20(2): 4–20.

Garrett, Charles. 2004. Chinatown, whose Chinatown? Defining America's
  borders with musical Orientalism. *Journal of the American Musicological
  Society* 57(1): 119–173.

Han, Kuo-Huang. 1978. The Chinese concept of program music. *Asian Music*
  X(1): 17–38.

———. 1985. Titles and program notes in Chinese musical repertoires.
  World of Music XXVII(1): 69–75.

———. 1989. Folk songs of the Han Chinese: Characters and classifica-
  tions. *Asian Music* 20(2): 107–128.

Huang, Jinpei. 1989. Xipi and erhuang of Beijing and Guangdong operas.
  Asian Music 20(2): 152–195.

Hwang, David Henry. 1989. *M Butterfly.* New York: Penguin Books.

Jones, Stephen. 1989. The golden-character scripture: Perspectives on Chinese melody. *Asian Music* 20(2): 21–66.

———. 1995. *Folk music of China: Living instrumental traditions.* New York
  and Oxford: Oxford University Press.

Kagan, Alan. 1963. Music and the Hundred Flowers Movement. *Musical
  Quarterly* 49: 417–430.

Lam, Joseph. 1996. Ritual and musical politics in the court of Ming Shi-
  zong. In *Harmony and counterpoint: Ritual music in Chinese context,* edited
  by B. Yung, E. S. Rawski and R. S. Watson. Stanford, CA: Stanford University Press. 35–53.

Lau, Frederick. 1995. "Lost in Time?" Sources of 20th century *dizi* repertory. *Pacific Review of Ethnomusicology* 7: 31–56.

Liang, Mingyue. 1985. *Music of the billion: An introduction to Chinese musical culture.* New York: Heinrichshofen Edition.

Lui, Tsun-yuen. 1968. A short guide to Ch'in. *Selected Reports* 1(2): 179–204.

McDougall, Bonnie, ed. 1984. *Popular Chinese literature and performing arts in the People's Republic of China, 1949–1979.* Berkeley: University of California Press.

Mittler, Barbara. 1997. *Dangerous tunes: The politics of Chinese music in Hong Kong, Taiwan, and the People's Republic of China since 1949 (Opera sinologica). 3.* Wiesbaden: Harrassowitz.

Myers, John. 1992. *The way of the pipa: Structure and imagery in Chinese lute music.* Kent, OH: Kent State University Press.

Perris, Arnold. 1983. Music as propaganda: Art at the command of doctrine in the People's Republic of China. *Ethnomusicology* 27(1): 1–28.

Provine, Robert C., Yoshihiko Tokumaru, and J. Lawrence Witzleben. 2002. *East Asia: China, Japan, and Korea (Garland encyclopedia of world music v. 7).* New York: Routledge.

Rees, Helen. 2000. *Echoes of history: Naxi music in modern China.* New York and London: Oxford University Press.

So, Jenny F. 2000. *Music in the age of Confucius.* Washington, DC, and Seattle: Freer Gallery of Art and Arthur M. Sackler Gallery Smithsonian Institution; distributed by the University of Washington Press.

Thrasher, Alan. 1985. The melodic structure of jiangnan sizhu. *Ethnomusicology* 29(2): 237–263.

———. 2000. *Chinese musical instruments (Images of Asia).* New York: Oxford University Press.

Tuohy, Sue. 2001. The sonic dimensions of nationalism in modern China: Musical representation and transformation. *Ethnomusicology* 45(1): 107–131.

Witzleben, Lawrence. 1995. *Silk and bamboo music in Shanghai: The jiangnan sizhu instrumental ensemble tradition.* Kent, OH: Kent State University Press.

Yung, Bell. 1985. *Da pu:* the recreative process for the music of the seven-string zither. In *Music and context: Essays in honor of John M. Ward,* edited by A. Shapiro. Cambridge, MA: Department of Music, Harvard University, 370–384.

Video

Bhattacharya, Deben, Denny Densham, Gour Karmakar, Adim Lundin, Jharna Bose, OET Foundation for Culture, Sussex Tapes (Firm), and Audio-Forum (Firm). 1992. *Performing arts of China: Instruments and music.* London and Guilford, CT: Sussex Tapes. Distributed by Audio-Forum. Videocassette (27 min.).

Beijing opera masks: The face of Chinese tradition. 2002. Films for the Humanities & Sciences. ISBN number: 1-4213-0839-8.

Chinese cracker: The making of the Peony Pavilion. 2000. Films for the Humanities & Sciences. ISBN number: 0-7365-3762-7. Video of *kunqu* opera.

The education of a singer at the Beijing Opera. c. 1994. A film by Marie-Claire. Princeton, NJ: Films for the Humanities & Sciences (55 min.). This video provides an in-depth look at the process of how young students are trained in Beijing opera in contemporary China.

Farewell my concubine. 1993. Directed by Kaige Chen. Miramax Films in association with Maverick Picture Company and Tomson (HK) Films Co., Ltd. The story is about the lives of two Beijing opera stars with numerous scenes of Beijing opera performance.

The heavenly voice of China. c. 1987. Los Angeles: Center for Visual Anthropology, University of Southern California (23 min.). Documents the efforts of members of an amateur Chinese opera club in Los Angeles as they try to pass their art down to the next generation.

Heritage of Chinese opera: Chinese art films. 1978. Distributed by Chinese Art Films. Kwang Hwa Mass Communications (31 min.). Illustrates the distinguishing features of Chinese opera, including paucity of stage props, falsetto singing, symbolism in gait and gesture, face painting that reveals character, acrobatics, stylized and colorful costumes, and accompaniment by a small orchestra.

Introduction to Chinese musical instrument. 1992. Parkville, Australia: University of Melbourne, Institute of Education, ERC Media Services Unit (130 min. and teacher's guide). Each instrument is shown, the name is given in English and Chinese, and a musician demonstrates basic performing techniques and plays a typical solo piece. Concludes with a five-piece ensemble performance.

The JVC video anthology of world music and dance. 1988. East Asia/Producer, Ichikawa Katsumori (JVC) (255 min.).

No. 17 Cotton Mill Shanghai Blues: China. 1994. Shanachie (as part of The Beats of the Hearts Series).

Performing arts of China. 1987. Produced by Deben Bhattacharya. Mt. Vernon, NY: Distributed by Gould Media, Inc. (27 min.). Video about Chinese opera, minorities of the southwest opera, Chinese instrumental music, and Uyghurs on the Silk Route.

Performing arts of China: Folk music. 1983. London: OET Foundation for Culture (30 min.). Presents traditional folk songs and music of China,

including Mongolia, Suzhou, and Hangzhou. Shows how musical instruments are constructed and played. Explains the texts of some songs and
shows how stories are recited with music by traveling musicians. Also
describes the way of life in China.

Singing to remember. c. 1991. New York: Asian American Arts Centre. A por-
trait of Ng Sheung Chi, master singer of Cantonese storytelling known
as muk yu or mu yu. Mr. Ng, a recent immigrant to the United States,
discusses and performs the singing traditions of Toisan, his home village
in China.

Yellow earth. 1985. Directed by Kaige Chen. New York: Fox Lorber Home
Video. Shows village ritual, folk music, and northern-style wind and
percussion bands in procession.

Recording Companies

ROI Productions Ltd.
Flat B1, 23rd. floor, Prince Industrial Building
766 Prince Edward Road East
Sun Po Kong, Kowloon
Hong Kong
URL: http://www.dragons-music.com
email: roi@dragons-music.com
telephone: (852) 2897-9188
fax: (852) 2976-0098

Lyrichord Discs, Inc.
PO Box 1977
Old Chelsea Station
New York, NY 10011-1726
Phone: 212-929-8234 Fax: 212-929-8245
Email address: info@lyrichord.com

Ocora Radio France
tel 33 1 4230 3804
fax 33 14230 4949
URL: http://www.fnac.com/Shelf/default .asp?NID=1333499
Hugo Production (HK) Ltd.
URL: http://www.hugocd.com

Online Sources of Chinese Music

Pictures and short descriptions of common popular Chinese instruments:
http://chcp.org/music/Vmusic.html
http://www.paulnoll.com/China/Music/China-musical-instruments.html
http://www.chinesemusic.co.uk/english/pluckints.htm
http://www.gio.gov.tw/taiwan-website/av/sou_sig/sight04_6.htm

Heritage of Chinese opera: a good general introduction to Chinese opera focusing on staging, singing styles, costumes, and movements: http://www.gio.gov.tw/taiwan-website/av/sou_sig/sight04_6.htm

Chinese traditional music in Taiwan: a short video on Chinese music in Taiwan. The first part introduces Chinese instruments in Taiwan, the second part is about a kind of local wind and percussion music called *beiguan,* and the third part discusses the current state of Chinese music in Taiwan. Good closeups of instruments: http://www.gio.gov.tw/taiwan-website/av/sou_sig/sight04_18.htm

Index